GREAT ATHLETES

THE TWENTIETH CENTURY

GREAT ATHLETES

THE
TWENTIETH
CENTURY

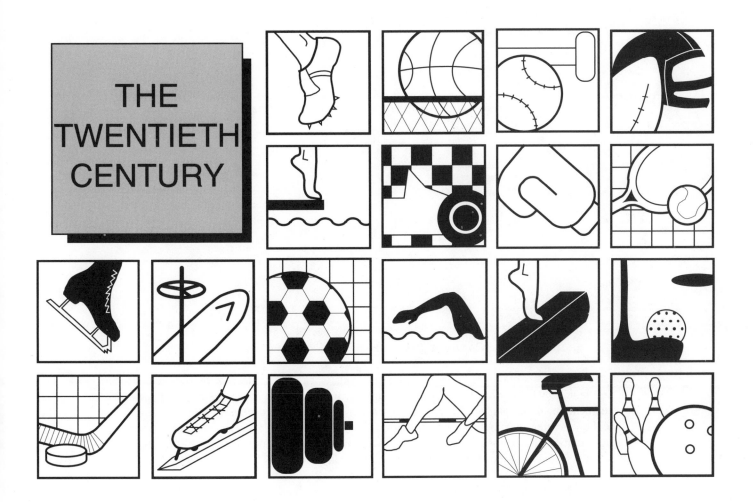

20   Wilson-Zurbriggen

A Magill Book
From The Editors of Salem Press

With special assistance from
The Amateur Athletic Foundation of Los Angeles'
Paul Ziffren Sports Resource Center

SALEM PRESS
Pasadena, California   Englewood Cliffs, New Jersey

Cover designed by David H. Hundley and Custom Graphics, Inc.
Photographs courtesy of the Paul Ziffren Sports Resource Center

Library of Congress Cataloging-in-Publication Data
Great athletes
    p. cm.—(The Twentieth Century)
  "A Magill book from the editors of Salem Press."
  Includes index.
    1. Athletes—Biography—Dictionaries. I. Salem Press. II. Series: Twentieth century (Pasadena, Calif.)
GV697.A1G68   1992
796'.092'2–dc20   91–32301
[B]   CIP
ISBN 0-89356-775-2 (set)
ISBN 0-89356-795-7 (volume 20)

First Printing

Contents

GREAT ATHLETES

THE
TWENTIETH
CENTURY

HACK WILSON

Sport: Baseball

Born: April 26, 1900
Elwood City, Pennsylvania
Died: November 23, 1948
Baltimore, Maryland

Early Life

Lewis Robert Wilson was born an illegitimate child on April 26, 1900, in the bleak mining town of Elwood City, Pennsylvania. Unhappy in his squalid home and with a poor record at school, he dropped out of the sixth grade to go to work in a print shop for four dollars a week. Seeking better wages, he found employment in a locomotive factory, a steel mill, and a shipyard, but what he enjoyed most was playing semiprofessional baseball whenever he could find a team that would let him be its catcher.

The Road to Excellence

It was dirty, painful work to crouch for several hours in the summer sun wearing heavy pads over a "wool flannel" uniform and being bruised by foul tips, hurtling baserunners, and fastballs banging into the thin leather of his borrowed catcher's mitt, yet the young Wilson thrived on it. Despite thin ankles and small feet (he wore a size 5½ shoe), he was developing a barrel chest and heavily muscled arms, and he could already hit the ball farther than most of the older men with whom he played.

In 1921, "Hack," as he had already been nicknamed, after a burly wrestler some of his pals thought he resembled, signed his first professional contract with a team in Martinsburg, West Virginia. A broken leg suffered while sliding home in his first game did not keep him sidelined for long, but, unable to bend the stiff limb so as to squat behind home plate, he began playing the outfield. Soon he realized it was his natural position. Batting .356 and .366 during his two years at Martinsburg, he was promoted for the 1923 season to Portsmouth, Virginia, where he hit a spectacular .388.

Near the end of the 1923 season, he was signed by the World Champion New York Giants. In 1924, he became their regular center fielder, replacing the notorious Casey Stengel and playing all seven World Series games that fall against Washington. New York manager John McGraw called Hack the greatest judge of fly balls he had seen since the fabulous Tris Speaker, who set the standard for center fielders in his prime. Nevertheless, when Hack, who had begun to spend much of his off the field time drinking whiskey with admiring fans, got off to a poor start in 1925, McGraw sent him to the American Association Toledo Mud Hens. There Hack's all-around ability impressed the astute Joe McCarthy, the manager of the rival Louisville Cardinals.

The Emerging Champion

Hired to manage the Chicago Cubs for the 1926 season, McCarthy persuaded the team's owners to purchase Hack's contract. The "li'l round man" did not disappoint his benefactor. Despite a continuing love affair with the bottle, Hack led the National League in home runs and walks, finished second in runs batted in, and was third in doubles. Largely because of his inspiring play, the Cubs, who had finished last the previous year,

ended the 1926 season in second place, only two games behind the Cardinals.

A right-handed hitter, Hack swung from his heels with one of the heaviest bats ever used by a major leaguer. He tied for the league lead in home runs in both 1927 and 1928 and ranked second and third in runs batted in, as McCarthy struggled to build a pennant winner around his stumpy star. In 1929 he did so.

The Cubs of 1929 were one of the most awesome teams in baseball history. With Hack leading the league with a spectacular 159 runs batted in, the Chicagoans finished ten games ahead of their nearest rivals. Hack, said his admiring manager, was the best outfielder in baseball. Despite drinking whiskey at all hours and once having to be sobered up in the clubhouse before a game by being plunged into a tub of ice water, the center fielder, according to his mentor, could hit, field, run, and throw with any player.

Continuing the Story

In the fourth game of the 1929 World Series, however, Hack lost a fly ball in the sun, enabling the Philadelphia Athletics to score three times en route to a 10-run rally that was the Series turning point. Sportswriters derisively dubbed him "Sunny boy" and blamed the Cub defeat on him, despite his .471 batting average for the five games.

Stung by the epithets of his critics, the "sawed-off" man had one of the finest seasons in 1930 that any ballplayer ever experienced. Batting an impressive .356, he hammered out 56 home runs, the most ever in National League history, and knocked in an almost unbelievable 190 runs, still a record for both major leagues.

Yet fate had a cruel awakening in store for the exuberant Wilson. Near the end of the 1930 season, the tolerant McCarthy was replaced as the Cubs' manager by the puritanical, no-nonsense Rogers Hornsby, whose aversion to Hack's dissipations led him to play the "little giant" in only 112 games in 1931. Dispirited and unwilling to abandon his dissolute habits in order to placate Hornsby, Hack hit only .261 with but 13 homers. At the end of the season, he was traded to Brooklyn.

Temporarily sobered and trimmed down for the 1932 season, Hack hit 23 home runs and had 123 runs batted in, to go with a respectable .297 batting average. It was his last significant season, however. In 1933, he was in and out of the Brooklyn lineup. Late in the following season, the Dodgers traded him to Philadelphia, where he hit only .100 in seven games and was released. He never played another big league game.

Hack's few remaining years were spent in menial jobs. He was a bartender in a saloon, a bouncer in a dance hall, and a maintenance man in a public park. He died, alone and almost penniless, at age forty-eight on November 23, 1948.

Summary

Despite a weakness for alcohol that limited his career to only six good years and eventually killed him, genial, uncomplicated Hack Wilson was one of the greatest players of baseball's "golden age." It seems unlikely that either one of his two records will soon be broken.

Norman B. Ferris

STATISTICS

Season	Games	At Bats	Hits	Doubles	Triples	Home Runs	Runs	Runs Batted In	Batting Average	Slugging Average
1923	3	10	2	0	0	0	0	0	.200	.200
1924	107	383	113	19	12	10	62	57	.295	.486
1925	62	180	43	7	4	6	28	30	.239	.422
1926	142	529	170	36	8	**21**	97	109	.321	.539
1927	146	551	175	30	12	**30**	119	129	.318	.579
1928	145	520	163	32	9	**31**	89	120	.313	.588
1929	150	574	198	30	5	39	135	**159**	.345	.618
1930	155	585	208	35	6	**56**	146	**190**	.356	**.723**
1931	112	395	103	22	4	13	66	61	.261	.435
1932	135	481	143	37	5	23	77	123	.297	.538
1933	117	360	96	13	2	9	41	54	.267	.389
1934	74	192	47	5	0	6	24	30	.245	.365
Totals	1,348	4,760	1,461	266	67	244	884	1,062	.307	.545

NOTE: Boldface indicates statistical leader.

HONORS AND AWARDS

1930	National League Most Valuable Player
1930	Major league record for the most runs batted in in a season (190)
1930	National League record for the most home runs in a season (56)
1979	National Baseball Hall of Fame

2782

LARRY WILSON

Born: March 24, 1938
Rigby, Idaho

Early Life

Lawrence Frank Wilson was born in Rigby, Idaho, on March 24, 1938. His father was a truck driver for the Utah Power and Light Company. When Larry was ten, his mother died. Larry's dad never remarried. Larry has said he owes much of his success to his father, who, alone, reared him and his brother John. At Rigby High School, Larry was a small but aggressive athlete. He won sixteen varsity letters and led Rigby to the state football championship. He excelled in track, setting state records in the high jump and high hurdles. The high school athletic field at Rigby has been named Larry Wilson Field.

The Road to Excellence

Larry enrolled at the University of Utah in 1956, at the request of his father. He continued to be successful as a high jumper in track as well as a two-way player on the football field. He learned to be aggressive and to have fun under two football coaches. Jack Curtice taught Larry the fun of the game, and Ray Nagel taught Larry the importance of outhitting one's opponent. Larry was used mostly as an offensive player. As a fullback he held many scoring records at Utah by the time he graduated in 1960. He earned third team All-American honors his senior year.

He was selected in the seventh round of the National Football League (NFL) draft by the St. Louis Cardinals with little fanfare. The Cardinals agreed to try Larry on defense when it seemed that he had little chance of making the team on offense.

The Emerging Champion

Larry thought he was going to be cut by the Cardinals after their final pre-season game in San Francisco. He even asked his wife Dee Ann to meet him in San Francisco so they could drive to Idaho together once the cut was official. To their surprise, he made the team and started at defensive safety in the opening regular season game. He continued to start at that position for the next thirteen years.

Wilson became famous for the safety blitz, designed especially for him by Cardinals defensive coach Chuck Drulis. Larry was also known as a fierce competitor. He wore only a single bar on his helmet for a face mask. His clearly visible crooked nose (from multiple fractures) and his missing front teeth conveyed to fans and opponents just how determined and aggressive he was. His familiar number 8 was seemingly everywhere on the field making plays. The deadly tackler and pass defender demonstrated great courage by playing against the Pittsburgh Steelers in 1965 with both hands in casts; he made a key interception that led to a Cardinals victory. In 169 games Wilson intercepted 52 passes for 800 yards and 5 touchdowns. He intercepted 3 passes in one game twice, led the NFL with 10 interceptions in 1966, and tied an NFL mark by making interceptions in 7 straight games.

Continuing the Story

Larry was a five-time All-NFL selection. He

played in eight Pro Bowl games. Considered the best NFL safety ever, Larry twice was named Cardinals Most Valuable Player between 1966 and 1968, and in 1966 finished second for the NFL Player of the Year Award. It was somehow fitting that in Larry's final game in 1972, he played with a painful cracked rib that required special wrapping. It would have been easy to quit, but that was just not Larry's style. He played in pain right to the very end of his career.

Wilson served as director of scouting for the Cardinals from 1973 to 1976 before being promoted to assistant director of operations. In 1980 he was named the club's director of professional personnel. Besides being selected to the NFL All-Pro Team of the 1960's and to the AFL-NFL 1960-1984 All-Star Team, Wilson in 1978 was elected to the Pro Football Hall of Fame. He and his first wife, Dee Ann, had two sons and one daughter. In 1980 Wilson married radio personality Nancy Drew. He also accepted a job as the general manager of the Cardinals in 1988, the year they moved to Phoenix.

Wilson's courage served to inspire his team-mates, and even his retirement provided a lasting benefit for the city of St. Louis. In the team's hometown, a dinner in his honor raised some $30,000 for the St. Louis Children's Hospital. Roughly $20,000 of the money was used to start the Larry Wilson Fund for children with special medical needs. The plight of crippled children has always been of concern to Larry. He has long been close to the problem. Jed Wilson, Larry and Dee Ann's oldest son, was born with a spinal defect that left him permanently paralyzed from the waist down.

Summary

Larry Wilson was a courageous and determined professional football player who overcame many obstacles to become one of the best players ever at his position. He was an inspirational player who became a fixture in the St. Louis community, working to raise money for handicapped children. In both his career and his retirement, Larry has exemplified the marks of a true champion.

Kevin R. Lasley

HONORS AND AWARDS

1960	College All-American
1963-64, 1966-71	NFL Pro Bowl Team
1963, 1966-69	All-NFL Team
1966	Halas Trophy
1970	NFL All-Pro Team of the 1960's
1978	Pro Football Hall of Fame
1985	AFL-NFL 1960-1984 All-Star Team
—	Uniform number 8 retired by the Phoenix Cardinals

DAVE WINFIELD

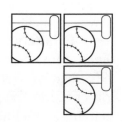

Sport: Baseball

Born: October 3, 1951
St. Paul, Minnesota

Early Life

David Mark Winfield was born on October 3, 1951, in St. Paul, Minnesota. His parents, Frank and Arline Winfield, were Minnesota natives. Dave was the younger of their two sons. By the time Dave was three, his parents separated. His father moved to the West Coast, while the rest of the family remained in St. Paul.

When Dave was about ten, he and his brother, Steve, became interested in baseball. They were not only fans but also avid players, participating in local youth leagues. Dave played third base and shortstop. Mrs. Winfield and her mother took a great interest in the boys' activities. They encouraged Dave and Steve not only to excel in sports but also to value hard work and education.

The Road to Excellence

By the time Dave entered high school in 1965, he was more than 6 feet tall. As a member of the school's baseball team, he pitched and played shortstop. American Legion baseball provided him with the opportunity to play during the summer.

At the end of his senior year of high school, in 1969, Dave's skill as a player provided him with choices. The Baltimore Orioles of the American League drafted him and assigned him to a minor league team. The University of Minnesota, Minneapolis, offered Dave a partial baseball scholarship, which provided a chance for a college education and the opportunity to play ball. He chose the scholarship.

Dave entered the University of Minnesota in 1969. He described himself as an unenthusiastic student, but in his second year, he began to take his class work seriously and declared a double major in black studies and political science. He studied hard and received good grades.

During his four years in college, Dave pitched for the baseball team and, during his freshman, junior, and senior years, he also played basketball. He received a full scholarship for basketball. In his senior year, the basketball team won the Big Ten Conference Championship and played in the National Invitational Tournament. The baseball team participated in the College World Series. Dave was named the tournament's most valuable player. For the season, he batted .385 and pitched for 13 wins and 1 loss.

The Emerging Champion

Dave's athletic ability had made him prominent by the end of his college career. In the spring of 1973, four professional sports teams selected him in their drafts. He was chosen as an outfielder by the San Diego Padres of the baseball National League, the Atlanta Hawks of the National Basketball Association, the Utah Stars of the American Basketball Association, and the Minnesota Vikings of the National Football League. The last selection was unusual because Dave had not played football in high school or in college.

Dave signed a contract with San Diego. He became a member of the Padres in 1973, bypassing the minor leagues. To develop his skills, he played winter baseball in Mexico after his first major league season.

2786

Between 1974 and 1977, Dave became an excellent professional baseball player. His talent was recognized in 1977 when he was named to the National League All-Star team for the first time.

In the 1970's, major league baseball's management adopted the policy of free agency. This allowed players with seven or more years of major league service who had fulfilled their contracts to sign contracts with other teams. Dave became a free agent after the 1980 season. He signed a ten-year agreement with the New York Yankees. As an outfielder for the Yankees from 1981 through 1988, Dave was named to the American League All-Star team each year. He won seven Gold Glove awards for excellence in fielding and four Silver Bat awards for his hitting.

An injury forced Dave to undergo back surgery after the 1988 season. He was unable to play baseball in 1989, but he was able to return to play the 1990 season as a newly signed member of the California Angels of the American League. After a slow start, Dave enjoyed a successful year. He batted 475 times and finished with a .267 batting average and 21 home runs. During the 1991 season, he accomplished the rare feat of hitting for the cycle—hitting a single, double, triple, and home run in the same game—in a 9-4 victory over the Kansas City Royals on June 24.

Continuing the Story

Dave never fit the image of the selfish professional athlete. Although he left the University of Minnesota without completing his bachelor's degree, he remained interested in education. In 1974, he established a scholarship and awards dinner for minority students in St. Paul.

Also in 1974, he began to buy blocks of tickets to Padres games, which were given to disadvantaged children. In 1977, after signing a new contract with San Diego, he created the David M. Winfield Foundation. At first, the Foundation purchased tickets to the annual All-Star games and gave them to children. In 1980, he committed the Foundation to spending money to provide physical examinations, health education, and health care for thousands of disadvantaged children.

After he had joined the Yankees in 1981, Dave moved the Foundation's offices to Fort Lee, New Jersey. His contract with the New York team required the Yankees to contribute $300,000 each year to the Winfield Foundation. Although there were some disagreements over the payments, Dave persisted, and the money was paid by the team.

In the middle of the 1980's, Dave and the Winfield Foundation's directors changed the focus of the organization. They were very concerned about the problem of drug abuse among young people. Dave appeared in a short film on drug abuse prevention, and the Foundation sponsored a program called the Drug Awareness Program, which made educational presentations in schools.

Summary

Dave Winfield's contributions to sports and to American society have been extensive. He took advantage of the opportunities his athletic talents provided to win college scholarships, obtain an education, and pursue a successful career in professional baseball. His success enabled him to assist many young people through his charitable foundation.

Ann M. Scanlon

STATISTICS

Season	Games	At Bats	Hits	Doubles	Triples	Home Runs	Runs	Runs Batted In	Batting Average	Slugging Average
1973	56	141	39	4	1	3	9	12	.277	.383
1974	145	498	132	18	4	20	57	75	.265	.438
1975	143	509	136	20	2	15	74	76	.267	.403
1976	137	492	139	26	4	13	81	69	.283	.431
1977	157	615	169	29	7	25	104	92	.275	.467
1978	158	587	181	30	5	24	88	97	.308	.499
1979	159	597	184	27	10	34	97	**118**	.308	.558
1980	162	558	154	25	6	20	89	87	.276	.450
1981	105	388	114	25	1	13	52	68	.294	.464
1982	140	539	151	24	8	37	84	106	.280	.560
1983	152	598	169	26	8	32	99	116	.283	.513
1984	141	567	193	34	4	19	106	100	.340	.515
1985	155	633	174	34	6	26	105	114	.275	.471
1986	154	565	148	31	5	24	90	104	.262	.462
1987	156	575	158	22	1	27	83	97	.275	.457
1988	149	559	180	37	2	25	96	107	.322	.530
1990	132	475	127	21	2	21	70	78	.267	.453
1991	150	568	149	27	4	28	75	86	.262	.472
Totals	2,551	9,464	2,697	460	80	406	1,459	1,602	.285	—

NOTE: Boldface indicates statistical leader.

HONORS AND AWARDS

1973	College World Series Most Outstanding Player
1973	*The Sporting News* College Baseball All-American
1977-80	National League All-Star Team
1979-80	National League Gold Glove
1981-88	American League All-Star Team
1981-84	American League Silver Bat Award
1982-85, 1987	American League Gold Glove
1987	Honorary Doctor of Laws, Syracuse University

HANS WINKLER

Sport: Equestrian

Born: July 24, 1926
Barmen, Germany

Early Life

Hans Günter Winkler was born July 24, 1926, in Barmen, a small town near Dortmund, Germany. His father, Paul Winkler, was an equerry and riding instructor, but he wanted his son to follow another career, such as business.

From earliest childhood, however, Hans Winkler was interested in horses and horsemanship, and, by the time he was thirteen, he had managed to participate in several competitions and horse shows.

When World War II broke out in 1939, the Winkler family moved to Frankfurt, where the father managed a small riding academy and Hans managed to spend time every day with horses. He decided he would make showjumping his specialty. He had hoped to continue his early training since, because of his age, no one believed he would have to serve in the military. In 1944, however, at the age of eighteen, he was drafted and immediately sent to the Eastern Front, which was already collapsing under the Soviet advance. His father, who had been drafted earlier, was killed on the Western Front a week before the war ended.

Captured and imprisoned in eastern Germany, Hans managed to escape and made his way back to Frankfurt, where he finally found his mother in the almost completely destroyed city. Ill from the hardships of the prison camp, suffering from hepatitis, with no money, hardly any food, and with a mother to support, Hans Winkler was still determined to pursue a career as an equestrian.

The Road to Excellence

Although pursuing such a career seemed impossible in impoverished, bombed-out postwar Germany, Hans Winkler was fortunate in meeting the stable master for the Landgrave of Hesse, who invited Winkler to work for him at Friedrichshof Castle near Frankfurt. There Hans stayed for two years, gaining valuable experience. He met a young woman from Frankfurt, the daughter of a successful textile merchant, who suggested to Hans that they set up a stable of horses for performing in competitions and horse shows.

Hans Winkler always felt his success was to a large extent the result of his ability to understand horses. Through kindness and patient training, he could coax a performance out of horses with severe nervous problems and other handicaps. Because of this ability, he felt he could buy with his limited funds three horses that were considered to be ruined because of misuse or nervous problems. He participated in a number of competitions and horse shows so successfully that he managed to pay off his debts.

More important, Hans and his horses attracted the attention of Dr. Gustav Rau, the director of DOKR, the German Olympic Committee for horsemanship. In 1951, Dr. Rau invited Hans to come to Warendorf in northwest Germany, near the Dutch border, where the committee had its stables. At first, the situation at Warendorf was difficult. Hans faced considerable competition and even jealousy. Yet that first year, he won twenty-four first prizes and twenty-three second and third prizes in local competitions and shows. In spite of these successes, Hans knew that with-

out a first-rate horse, he would never achieve his goal of becoming a champion showjumper.

The Emerging Champion

In 1950, Hans had ridden a young mare named Halla. Because she was temperamental, nervous, and inclined to buck, her owner wanted to get rid of her. The year that Hans came to Warendorf, Halla's owner offered her to the German Olympic Committee, but after several performances, they declared the horse unfit to train for the Olympics. The owner again approached Hans, who, firmly believing she had championship qualities, decided to try to train her. The work was difficult, but gradually he developed an understanding with the nervous but intelligent animal. Halla, said Hans, was the greatest thing that ever happened to him. It was she who enabled him to become a champion.

The months of patient training paid off. Hans, riding Halla, became World Riding Champion in 1954 and 1955. The following year at the Olympics in Stockholm, Hans and Halla won the gold medal in the individual showjumping event and in the team event. Involving as it does enlarged obstacles and a close working relationship with two other team members, winning a team event is as difficult and as important as winning an individual event.

Winning both the individual and team event was a great psychological boost not only for Hans but also for the Germans. Because of the war, they had only recently been allowed to take part in the Olympics.

Continuing the Story

In 1957, Hans, riding Halla, became the European Riding Champion. Because of an injury, he could not defend his showjumping title at the 1960 Olympics, although he was a participant in the team event, again winning the gold medal. That same year, Halla made her last winning jump, having completed 125 showjumps, a record for a German horse. In gratitude, Winkler wrote a book, *Halla: Die Geschichte ihrer Laufbahn* (1960; Halla: the history of her career).

By 1964, Hans Winkler had been a winner in nearly one thousand events, including five hundred international events. He participated in the Olympic Games until 1976, when his team won a silver medal in the team event. Hans Winkler is considered the world's most successful Olympic showjumping rider and is the only rider in Olympic history to win five gold medals. Although he retired from competition jumping, he remained active in the equestrian area both through teaching and business activities. His leisure activities include skiing and hunting. Hans Winkler made his home in Warendorf; he has been married twice.

Summary

Hans Winkler's brilliant career as an equestrian and showjumper is proof not only that hard work and perseverance can achieve success despite great obstacles but also that kindness to and understanding of the horses can be a major factor in bringing about the success.

Nis Petersen

MAJOR CHAMPIONSHIPS

Year	Competition	Event	Place
1954-55	World Riding Championship	—	1st
1956	Olympic Games	Individual jumping	Gold
		Team event	Gold
1964, 1976	Olympic Games	Team event	Gold
1957	European Riding Championship	—	1st
1965, 1968	King George V Cup	—	1st
1968	Olympic Games	Team event	Bronze
1976	Olympic Games	Team event	Silver

HONORS AND AWARDS

1954	Needle of Honor, Senate of West Berlin
1956	Gold Band, German Sports Press Association
1960	Named Best Sportsman of the Decade
1964	Needle of Honor, International Riding Association
1974	Grand Cross of Honor, Federal Republic of Germany
1976	German Riding Association Award

KATARINA WITT

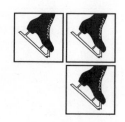

Sport: Figure skating

Born: December 3, 1965
Karl-Marx-Stadt (Chemnitz), East Germany

Early Life

Katarina Witt was born on December 3, 1965, in Karl-Marx-Stadt, now Chemnitz, in the German Federal Republic, which was then the German Democratic Republic, or East Germany. Katarina's father was the manager of an agriculture cooperative; her mother was a physical therapist. Her sister-in-law, Anett Pötzsch, was a figure skater who won the Olympic gold medal in 1980.

Katarina was fascinated by figure skating while still in kindergarten. At the age of five, she persuaded her parents to let her try the sport. In her own words, the first time on ice she said, "This is for me," and decided to make figure skating her life's work.

The Road to Excellence

Bernd Egert, the head coach of the Karl-Marx-Stadt Sports Club and School, one of the best in East Germany, by chance saw Katarina skating and was so impressed by her performance that he enrolled her in the school's intensive training program.

The training was strict and demanded the complete attention of the trainee, but Katarina was an excellent pupil. She trained every day from seven in the morning until eight in the evening and spent more time with her coaches then she did with her family. She had no time for anything other than her training and no friends outside of those with whom she worked.

The work paid off. By the age of nine, Katarina had become so skillful that her talents were recognized by Jutta Müller, East Germany's most famous skating coach, who now took over the young girl's training and made her into a world-famous sports figure. Many have criticized East Germany's training system as too rigid and severe, but Katarina Witt maintains she could not have achieved her success in any other way.

The Emerging Champion

Under Jutta Müller's coaching, Katarina soon demonstrated her extraordinary skill, when, at the age of eleven, she made her first triple jump, a Salchow, involving rotating the body in mid-air. At the age of fourteen, she finished tenth in the world championship competition, and two years later, at the age of sixteen, she captured the European championship and placed second in the world championship.

In 1984, now nineteen, she achieved the world championship, defeating Rosalynn Sumners of the United States, a two-time national champion. Katarina's greatest triumph, however, which made her a world star, was her amazing performance that same year at the Winter Olympics held in Sarajevo, Yugoslavia, where she again defeated Rosalynn Sumners to capture the gold medal. What impressed the judges was not only Katarina's skating but also her artistic ability combined with a radiant personality and natural beauty. An observer commented that her performance was a perfect blend of athleticism and art. It so impressed the viewers that Katarina received more than 35,000 love letters.

2794

Continuing the Story

After Sarajevo, Katarina Witt's triumphs continued; she now was first in the field of women's figure skating. In the World Championships held in March, 1985, in Tokyo, she defeated Kira Ivanova of the Soviet Union, thereby preventing Soviet skaters from capturing all the top titles. Katarina skated to the music of George Gershwin, landing each of her triples smoothly in perfect time with the music.

In 1986, Katarina lost the World Championships to the American contender, Debi Thomas, the first African-American woman to gain the title. The following year, Katarina regained her title after a fierce contest with Thomas, perfectly completing five triple-jumps and two double axels and receiving top ratings from seven of the nine judges. To win that contest, Katarina claimed she had trained harder than she ever had before. Even Debi Thomas had to admit that her rival was amazing: "She's tough, she just goes out there and does what she has to."

The two superstars competed again in February, 1988, at the Winter Olympics in Calgary, Canada, in what was known as "The Battle of the Carmens." Both skated to the music of *Carmen*, an opera by the French composer Georges Bizet. The contest was close, but what won the gold medal for Katarina was her artistic interpretation of the opera's heroine. For two years, Katarina had studied acting, and, as a critic noted, Thomas skated brilliantly to the music but Katarina became Carmen. Some skating fans were irritated because they thought Katarina relied too much on her radiant good looks, her acting ability, and her beautiful costumes, thereby unfairly influencing the judges. Katarina defended her performance, saying one should stress what one has and what is attractive.

Katarina Witt again won the World Championships title at the competition held less than a month after Calgary in Budapest, Hungary. Although Katarina had many offers from foreign countries, including the United States, to skate professionally, appear on stage, or become a model, she preferred to stay in Germany, grateful for the excellent training she had received free of charge. She planned to continue training as an actress, which she hopes will become her second career. She does not want to be remembered only as a figure skater.

Summary

In her short but brilliant career, Katarina Witt won the European Championships in figure skating six times, the World Championships four times, and the Olympic gold medal twice. She is proof of what talent, inspiration, excellent training, and hard work can do. Possibly Katarina's greatest contribution to figure skating is that, through her acting ability, the use of music, and the careful selection of costumes, she has helped raise an athletic event to an art form.

Nis Petersen

2796

MAJOR CHAMPIONSHIPS

Year	Competition	Place
1980	European Championships	13th
1980	World Championships	10th
1981	European Championships	5th
1981	World Championships	5th
1982	European Championships	2d
1982	World Championships	2d
1983	European Championships	1st
1983	World Championships	4th
1984	European Championships	1st
1984	Olympic Games	Gold
1984	World Championships	1st
1985	European Championships	1st
1985	World Championships	1st
1986	European Championships	1st
1986	World Championships	2d
1987	European Championships	1st
1987	World Championships	1st
1988	European Championships	1st
1988	Olympic Games	Gold
1988	World Championships	1st

WILLIE WOOD

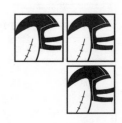

Sport: Football

Born: December 23, 1936
Washington, D.C.

Early Life

William Vernell Wood was born in Washington, D.C., on December 23, 1936. Both of his parents worked for the federal government. Willie was not interested in a career, in sports, or in school as a youngster. Instead, he joined a gang and spent most of his time hanging around on street corners in Washington. His gang sometimes got into fights with groups of boys from other neighborhoods.

Willie's amazing story does not end here. Fortunately, his situation began to improve. A boy's club opened up just a block from his house, and one of the counselors there took a special liking to him. Suddenly, sports became a new way of life for Willie.

The Road to Excellence

Willie became a good athlete at Armstrong High School in Washington, but his grades were not good enough for him to attend college, and he was forced to turn down scholarships. He attended Coalinga Junior College in Southern California, and moved on to the University of Southern California (USC). He played both quarterback and defensive back for the USC Trojans, although he sat out part of his junior and senior seasons because of a shoulder separation. He was used primarily on defense in his last year and drew little attention from professional football teams.

Willie was not offered a job by any National Football League (NFL) team. Yet he knew he wanted to try to play professionally, and he did not give up on his dream. He sat down and wrote letters to all the teams in the league. Only the Green Bay Packers wrote back, offering him the chance to try out.

The Emerging Champion

Willie was only 5 feet 10 inches and about 170 pounds, so when he came in for his physical he hid weights in his socks so that no one would find out how light he really was.

Despite the odds against him, Willie made the team. Just making the team, however, was not enough for him. He wanted to be a starter. The only way an unknown rookie could prove himself to the coaches was by making the most of whatever opportunities arose. Wood became a standout player on the special teams. He became known as a fierce tackler, and his speed helped him to become an excellent punt returner. By the time he began his second season with the team, the coaches were convinced, and Willie had become a starter in the defensive backfield.

In his second season, he led the league in punt returns. A year later, he led the league in interceptions, with 9, and was on his way to stardom. In each of his first three seasons, he helped the Packers reach the NFL Championship Game. Because he was small and had no special college reputation to speak of, Willie had to use every means at his disposal to succeed. His devotion was such that he did anything necessary to help the team.

Continuing the Story

Willie was a gifted athlete, with great speed

2798

and jumping ability. He was also a smart player. Because he had played quarterback in high school and in college, on defense he tried to outthink the other team's quarterback, anticipating the next play. His ability to guess what might happen next helped him get many of his 48 career interceptions.

One of Willie's most important interceptions helped the Packers win the first Super Bowl. Green Bay was the champion of the more established NFL, while their opponents, the Kansas City Chiefs, were from the newer American Football League (AFL). Many fans felt that it would be embarrassing for the Packers if they lost, or even if the game was close. Early in the second half, with his team ahead only 14-10, Willie intercepted a pass. He scooted down the sidelines and set up a touchdown that gave the Packers a 21-10 lead. Green Bay won the game, 35-10.

He was not famous only for his speed on interceptions and punt returns. He worked out with weights to build himself up, eventually getting his playing weight up to 190 pounds. In time, he became a punishing tackler.

Willie had a very successful career, helping the Packers win the first two Super Bowls. After his playing days were over, he remained in demand as a coach. He joined the San Diego Chargers as an assistant coach the year after he retired as a player. Eventually, he became a head coach with a team in the World Football League, a rival organization. After that league folded, Wood worked his way up through the ranks of assistant coaches to become the first African-American head coach in the history of the Canadian Football League.

Summary

Few observers gave Willie Wood any chance of making it in professional football. Once he did, they said he had no chance to become a star. Willie fooled them all. He had to overcome many obstacles: a bad start as a youth, an injury that hurt his professional chances, and a lack of great size. Yet he never gave up, and he kept working hard even after he had become a star in the NFL.

John McNamara

HONORS AND AWARDS

1962, 1965, 1967-69	*The Sporting News* Western Conference All-Star Team
1963, 1965-71	NFL Pro Bowl Team
1963-68	NFL All-Pro Team
1970-71	*The Sporting News* NFC All-Star Team
1970	NFL All-Pro Team of the 1960's
1989	Pro Football Hall of Fame

LYNETTE WOODARD

Sport: Basketball

Born: August 12, 1959
Wichita, Kansas

Early Life

Lynette Woodard was born on August 12, 1959, in Wichita, Kansas, the youngest in a family that included three sisters and one brother.

Lynette became excited about basketball at an early age as she watched her cousin, Geese Ausbie, perform his Harlem Globetrotter ballhandling tricks. At age five she began to practice what she saw him do and spent a lot of time playing basketball.

The Road to Excellence

While in high school, Lynette led her Wichita North High basketball team to two state championships. Having grown to a height of six feet by the end of her high school career, she was highly recruited by college coaches. Coach Marian Washington convinced her to attend the University of Kansas in 1977.

Though only a freshman, Lynette quickly established herself as one of the country's top players. She led the nation in rebounding her first year and was named Freshman of the Year by two nationwide publications. In 1979, she followed her nation-leading rebound feat by leading the nation in scoring with a 31.7-points-per-game average. On January 6, 1981, Lynette Woodard broke the women's career scoring record of 3,199 points when she scored the first basket in a home contest against Stephen F. Austin College. Lynette also led the nation in steals for three years.

The Emerging Champion

Her Kansas career was filled with accomplishment after accomplishment. By the time she graduated with a speech communications degree in 1981, Lynette held eight University of Kansas career records, seven single-season records, and five single-game records. Four times she was named a Kodak All-American and twice an Academic All-American, matching her hardwood performances with dedication in the classroom. Lynette was recognized as the nation's best collegiate female basketball player when she won the Wade Trophy in 1981. During her career, the Kansas Jayhawks compiled a 108-32 record. Her accomplishments were recognized by her alma mater when she became the first woman to be inducted into the university's Athletic Hall of Fame. She also received the National Collegiate Athletic Association (NCAA) Today's Top Five Award in 1982.

Before her collegiate career ended, Lynette was also becoming an international basketball sensation. Her scoring and rebounding abilities made her an asset for the United States teams. She played on three United States teams in 1978 and 1979, including the gold medal-winning 1979 World University Games team. She was also selected for the 1980 Olympic team that did not play when the United States chose to boycott the Moscow Olympics. The boycott was a disappointment for Lynette and for all the players who had trained so hard for the games.

Following graduation, Lynette continued her career in a women's professional basketball league in Skio, Italy. After a year overseas, she returned

2801

to the United States and played on the 1983 Pan-American gold medal-winning U.S. team and World University Games silver medal-winning team. Lynette again became an Olympian in 1984, and this time she captained the U.S. squad that won the gold medal at the Olympics in Los Angeles.

Continuing the Story

Where to play after the Olympics was the question facing Lynette. She became an assistant coach at the University of Kansas. But in 1983, Lynette saw a newspaper ad saying the Harlem Globetrotters would be holding tryouts to select one woman to sign as a Globetrotter. Two tryout camps were held in late summer and early fall of 1985. Eighteen women, the nation's best, were selected for the tryouts. When the tryouts were finished and the player was chosen, Lynette's lifelong dream had come true: She would become a Globetrotter.

Lynette's cousin Geese was no longer a member of the team, and the other members were a bit unsure of Lynette at first. They figured her selection might be just a publicity stunt. Geese encouraged her from afar, though, and Lynette's talent and outgoing personality helped to win the quick approval of her male teammates. Lynette had little time to adjust herself, as she played her first game with the Globetrotters in Brisbane, Australia, just ten days after joining the team. Thus began a schedule that would include almost 200 games a year and a series of "firsts" for her and for the Globetrotters: her first game as a Globetrotter in the United States; her first live television appearance with the team; her first game in her hometown of Wichita as a Globetrotter. Lynette enjoyed playing for fun and making people laugh. The fans also seemed to enjoy seeing her perform with the team.

In October, 1987, Lynette announced that her lifelong dream of being a Globetrotter had been fulfilled and, after two years, it was time to move on. Lynette's two-year contract expired before the season, and terms of a new contract could not be worked out to her satisfaction. The major roadblock in the contract negotiations was the Globetrotters policy limiting the players' outside projects, particularly promotions. Lynette felt her contract was too binding and that it was in her best interest to leave the Globetrotter organization. Lynette's upcoming projects would include an instructional basketball video, speaking engagements, camps, and clinics. She would again serve as a Kansas assistant coach in the 1989-90 season and professionally in Japan.

Summary

Lynette Woodard's career has demonstrated that dreams can come true. From the age of five, she dreamed of becoming a Harlem Globetrotter. As a collegian, she became one of the all-time greats in the women's game, propelling herself into a tryout and eventual selection as the first female player for the Globetrotters.

Rita S. Wiggs

STATISTICS

Season	Games	Field Goals	Field Goal Percentage	Free Throws	Free Throw Percentage	Rebounds	Assists	Total Points	Scoring Average
1977-78	33	366	.497	101	.664	490	47	833	25.2
1978-79	38	519	.562	139	.656	545	97	1,177	31.7
1979-80	37	372	.504	137	.714	389	165	881	23.8
1980-81	30	305	.533	122	.693	281	196	732	24.5
Totals	138	1,562	.526	499	.682	1,705	505	3,623	26.3

MILESTONES

★ The first female athlete to win the NCAA Today's Top Five Award

HONORS AND AWARDS

1978	*Street and Smith's* College Freshman of the Year
1978-81	All-Big Eight Conference Team
1978-81	Kodak All-American
1978	University of Kansas Athletic Hall of Fame
1979	U.S. World University Games Gold Medalist
1979-81	Big Eight Conference Tournament Most Valuable Player
1980	Women's U.S. Olympic Basketball Team
1980-81	Academic All-American
1981	*Street and Smith's* College Basketball Co-Player of the Year
1981	Broderick Award
1981	Wade Trophy
1982	NCAA Today's Top Five Award
1982	National Association for the Advancement of Colored People Woman of the Year
1983	U.S. World University Games Silver Medalist
1983	U.S. Pan-American Games Gold Medalist
1984	U.S. Olympic Gold Medalist
1985	NCAA Salute to the 1984 U.S. Olympians
1986	Women's Sports Foundation Professional Sportswoman of the Year
1989	Big Eight Conference Player of the Decade
1989	National High School Sports Hall of Fame

JOHN WOODEN

Sport: Basketball

Born: October 14, 1910
Hall, Indiana

Early Life

John Robert Wooden was born on October 14, 1910, in Hall, Indiana. He lived his early days on farms in the local rural area. There was no running water or electricity in the Wooden home. John was the third of six children in a close, hardworking family. John's father was a strong and steady influence in his life. He was a stern but caring man who instilled discipline and honesty in John. John and his brothers were fond of playing a form of basketball with a rag ball and a tomato basket nailed to the hay loft in the barn.

The Road to Excellence

During the depression of the 1930's, John's father lost the family farm, and the family moved to Martinsville, Indiana, where John attended high school. At Martinsville he met Nellie, his wife to be. His high school basketball coach was Glenn Curtis (a man he would later succeed as Indiana State University's basketball coach). As a sophomore, John once quit the team over Curtis' treatment of certain favorite players. John later said that incident taught him to listen to players who disagreed with him as a coach. John went on to win all-state honors in basketball three straight years while excelling in baseball as well. He led the basketball team to a state championship in 1927.

After high school, John enrolled at Purdue University in West Lafayette, Indiana. There, he captained the 1932 National Collegiate Athletic

Association (NCAA) championship team. John, a scrappy 5-foot 10-inch guard, was named All-American three times; he is one of the few people named to the Naismith Memorial Basketball Hall of Fame as both a player and a coach.

After graduating from Purdue in 1932, John began teaching at Dayton High School in Kentucky, where he was the coach for all sports. At Dayton, he experienced his only losing season as a coach, an experience from which he later said he learned much. From Dayton, John returned to his native Indiana to coach at Central High School in South Bend. In eleven years of high school basketball coaching, he compiled an overall won-lost record of 218-42.

During that time his coaching career was interrupted by three years with the Navy in World War II. Wooden went on to serve as athletic director at Indiana State University in Terre Haute. For two years, John coached basketball and baseball. Then he headed west for the University of California at Los Angeles (UCLA) in 1948.

The Emerging Champion

In his first two years at UCLA, John built and trained a fine team. That group of basketball players won the Pacific Coast Conference (PCC) championship in 1950 for Wooden. The UCLA Bruins marched to the PCC title again in 1952 and 1956, but Wooden's success within his own conference was only part of the story.

John's first really great team emerged in 1963-64. The heart of the team was a pair of scrappy, sharpshooting guards named Walt Hazzard and Gail Goodrich. The team was unranked in the

2805

pre-season polls, but the Bruins swept to a 30-0 season and the National Collegiate Athletic Association (NCAA) championship.

Goodrich was back the following season, but the Bruins lost their first game. The team then rallied to sweep its second national crown in a row. In the NCAA final, Goodrich scored 42 of the Bruins' 91 points, and UCLA knocked out the University of Michigan 91-80.

The UCLA team had an off-year in 1965-66, but as coach, John had a banner season in recruiting. He landed the greatest collection of new basketball talent ever assembled at one school. His prize player was 7-foot 2-inch Lew Alcindor (who later became Kareem Abdul-Jabbar) of New York, the most sought-after high school player in the nation. John also landed a sharpshooting guard named Lucius Allen. For forwards, he recruited a pair of 6-foot 8-inch players, Lynn Shackleford and Mike Lynn.

From 1966 to 1968, Wooden's Bruins had a 47-game winning streak. The streak was finally snapped by the University of Houston, sparked by Elvin Hayes, in a game at Houston's Astrodome. Alcindor was injured and did not play well in the game, which was the team's only loss; the Bruins finished the season with a 29-1 record. UCLA enjoyed revenge against Houston in the NCAA Tournament, defeating the Cougars 101-69. The Bruins' victory over the University of North Carolina gave them another NCAA championship.

In 1969, the Alcindor-led Bruins became the first team to win three straight NCAA titles. They beat John's alma mater, Purdue, in the championship game.

Continuing the Story

John seemed long overdue to come off his winning streak. With the graduation of the awesome Alcindor, many thought UCLA's reign was finished, yet the coach had a few more tricks for his rivals. The next season, Alcindor's understudy, Steve Patterson, had the help of sophomore forwards Sidney Wicks and Curtis Rowe, and the Bruins captured their fourth straight NCAA crown in 1970. The trio of Patterson, Rowe, and Wicks came back in 1971 to win a fifth straight title.

The next year, Wooden built his team around another outstanding center, Bill Walton. UCLA went undefeated in 1971-72 and 1972-73, and captured two more NCAA championships. UCLA's win streak was finally stopped by Notre Dame in January, 1974, at a record 88. That year, the Bruins were at last defeated in NCAA Tournament play. They dropped a double-overtime thriller to North Carolina State in the national semifinals.

In 1975, UCLA captured its tenth national crown under John. He announced his retirement to the team before the final game against Kentucky, and the Bruins gave their coach a going-away present. They defeated the Wildcats 92-85.

There is little doubt about Wooden's coaching genius. Whatever kind of team he had, he managed to produce a winner.

In his career at UCLA, Wooden won 80 percent of his games. He coached more than a dozen players who went on to play professional basketball.

Summary

John Wooden has spoken to many people since he retired about how he achieved so much success. He states that "Success is peace of mind, which is a direct result of self-satisfaction in knowing you did your best to become the best that you are capable of becoming." John believes that attaining success is like the process of building a pyramid, only each block is a character trait such as discipline, faith, or patience. John continues to be an inspiration to his former athletes and to those who admire him as a successful leader.

Kevin R. Lasley

2807

STATISTICS

Season	Games	Field Goals	Free Throws	Free Throw Percentage	Total Points	Scoring Average
1929-30	13	45	26	—	116	8.9
1930-31	17	53	54	.693	140	8.2
1931-32	18	79	61	.709	219	12.2
Totals	48	177	141	—	475	9.9

MILESTONES

★ John Wooden's coaching record in NCAA Tournament play includes sixteen appearances, twelve Final Four appearances, and ten championship titles, for an overall won-lost record of 47-10

★ His overall NCAA coaching record (including NCAA Tournament games) is 664-162, for an .804 winning percentage

★ The only member of the Naismith Memorial Basketball Hall of Fame inducted both as a player and as a coach

HONORS AND AWARDS

1930-32	Helms Athletic Foundation All-American
1932	Citizens Savings College Basketball Player of the Year
1932	Big Ten Conference medal for outstanding achievement in scholarship and athletics
1960	Naismith Memorial Basketball Hall of Fame (as a player)
1964, 1967, 1969-70, 1972-73	United Press International Division I Coach of the Year
1964, 1967, 1970, 1972-73	U.S. Basketball Writers Association Division I Coach of the Year
1967, 1969-70, 1972-73	Associated Press Division I Coach of the Year
1969-70, 1972	National Association of Basketball Coaches Division I Coach of the Year
1970	*The Sporting News* Sportsman of the Year
1972	*Sports Illustrated* Co-Sportsman of the Year
1972	Naismith Memorial Basketball Hall of Fame (as a coach)
1974	John W. Bunn Award
1974	Awarded honorary doctorate in physical education by the Purdue University Board of Trustees for his outstanding contribution to coaching

CYNTHIA WOODHEAD

Sport: Swimming

Born: February 7, 1964
Riverside, California

Early Life

Cynthia Woodhead was born on February 7, 1964, in Riverside, California. Life in Riverside was happy for Cynthia as she grew up. She went to school with the other children her age, but, from an early age, a difference could be seen when she began to swim. Coaches noticed her special talent, and she got better and better. Her family and friends were supportive of her swimming. As Cynthia got older, she would have to go to practice before and after school in order to get in enough training for her grueling sport. She did not mind; she loved giving one hundred percent, as she had learned from her family from an early age. She believed that, in order to give anything an honest try, one must always try one's best.

The Road to Excellence

Cynthia emerged as a star swimmer in 1977, when she was thirteen. At the Amateur Athletic Union (AAU) short-course nationals, Cynthia finished third in both the 200- and 500-meter freestyle. Then, only three months later at the AAU long-course championships, she tied for second in the 200-meter freestyle and finished eighth in the 400 meters. She made the United States National Team and placed fourth in the 200-meter freestyle at a meet with the German Democratic Republic team.

Almost overnight, Cynthia became a champion. When the United States swam against the Soviet Union, she placed first in the 200-meter freestyle. Although she was swimming against girls who were older and more experienced than she was, her natural talent and determination carried her through. She had always felt that she was this good, and now she was getting a chance to prove it.

Cynthia did very well in her thirteenth year in 1978, winning races from as short as 100 yards to as long as 1,650 yards at many world-caliber meets. She swam at many international meets, including the AAU Championships and the World Championships.

The Emerging Champion

In 1978, Cynthia set her first world record in the 200-meter freestyle at the 1978 World Championships at the age of fourteen. When the swimming world began the 1979 season, no one person had any idea that Cynthia was going to take the world by storm. Her first major meet was the Women's International, where she earned a first in the 500-yard freestyle, a second in the 200-yard freestyle, third in the 1,650 yards, and fourth in the 100-meter freestyle. During this year, she set the world and American records in the 200-meter freestyle and the American record in the 200-yard freestyle, and dominated the middle-distance events. For the next two years, Cynthia seemed almost unstoppable in the middle-distance events. Watching her swim in races was an incredible sight; she was always at least a second or two ahead of the field.

In 1979, she won five national titles and took three gold medals in the Pan-American Games. During those games, she was also named Most

2809

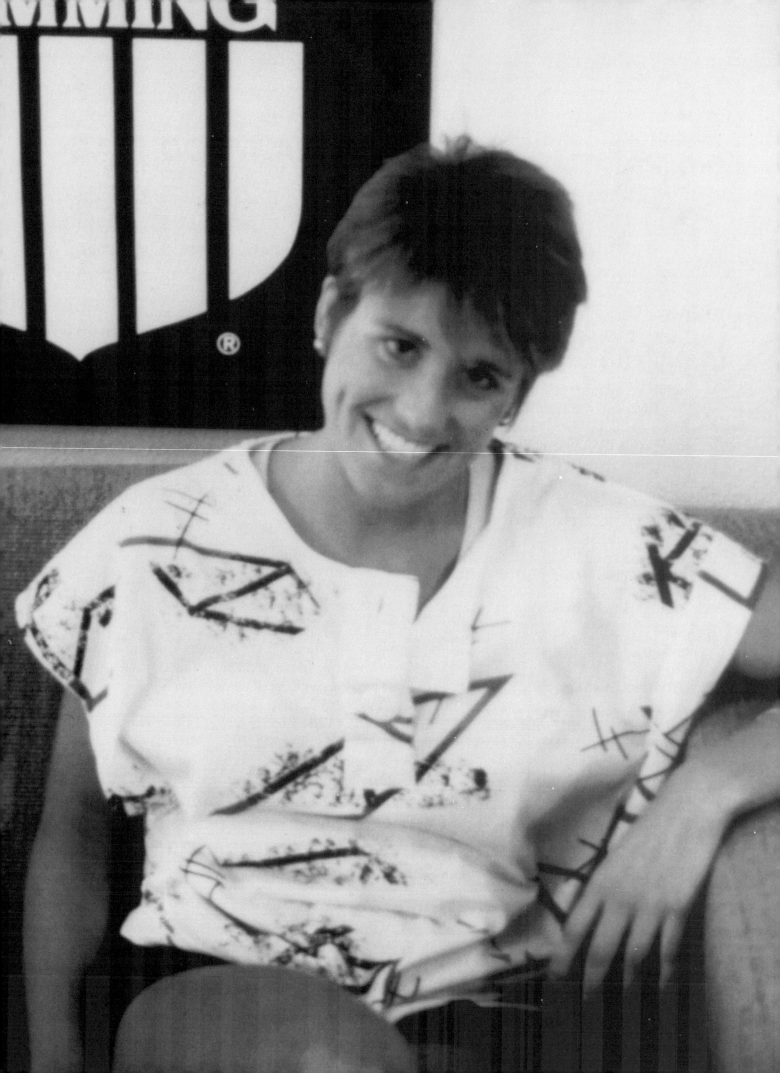

Valuable Player. She broke her existing world record in the 200-meter freestyle with a time of 1 minute 58.43 seconds. She then went on to win three more gold medals in middle-distance events in the FINA Cup International Swim Meet. Only a few weeks later, the young swimmer picked up five more gold medals at the World Cup in Tokyo, once again lowering her mark in the 200-meter freestyle, to 1 minute 58.23 seconds. Coach Riggs, her coach at the time, could not believe how hard she worked, but the hard work paid off.

In January, 1980, Cynthia helped the United States team to victory at the United States Women's National Meet with a first, second, and fourth place. In June of 1980 at Mission Viejo, California, she again won the 200-meter freestyle. The next month she won the 400-meter freestyle at the Santa Clara International Invitational Swimming Meet.

Continuing the Story

Just as it seemed that Cynthia could only win races, she began to lose, and the more she lost, the harder she trained; as she trained harder, she swam even worse.

It is difficult for an athlete to lose and not know why. Cynthia spent much time switching coaches and finally settled down with coach Mark Schubert.

She was known as a hard worker and worked harder than most male swimmers who had trained with Coach Schubert. She lowered her body fat percentage to a dangerously low 8 percent, believing that the more fit she was, the faster she would go. Only after she and Schubert figured out that Cynthia was training too hard did they ease off training. Once they eased off, her times began to come down and she began to win again. This development culminated with her win at the 1983 Pan-American Games and a silver medal at the Olympic Games in 1984. Even though she was viewed as over the hill by the public, she came back and showed them she could still swim as fast as she did before.

Cynthia had a difficult time believing that she was training too hard because she was brought up with a strong work ethic. If she had not had success herself with a lighter training load, she probably never would have believed it. There is a fine line in athletics between giving too little and giving too much, and champions seem to always discover it sooner or later.

Summary

Retirement seems to be inevitable when a swimmer goes into a slump for as long as Cynthia Woodhead did in 1980. Yet, Cynthia proved that, with the proper training and determination, it is possible to come back better than before.

Brooke K. Zibel

STATISTICS

Year	Competition	Event	Place	Time
1977	AAU Long Course	200m freestyle	Silver	—
1977	AAU Short Course	200m freestyle	Bronze	—
		500m freestyle	Bronze	—
1978	World Championships	200m freestyle	Gold	1:58.53 WR
		400m freestyle	Silver	4:07.15
		800m freestyle	Silver	8:29.35
		4 × 100m freestyle relay	Gold	3:43.43
		4 × 100m medley relay	Gold	4:08.21
1979	Pan-American Games	100m freestyle	Gold	52.22 PAR
		200m freestyle	Gold	1:58.43 WR, PAR
		400m freestyle	Gold	4:10.56 PAR
		4 × 100m freestyle relay	—	3:45.82
		4 × 100m medley relay	—	4:13.24
1983	Pan-American Games	200m freestyle	Gold	2:01.33
		400m freestyle	Gold	4:14.07
1984	Olympic Games	200m freestyle	Silver	—

NOTE: WR=World Record. PAR=Pan-American Record.

2812

GUMP WORSLEY

Sport: Ice hockey

Born: May 14, 1929
Montreal, Quebec, Canada

Early Life

Lorne John "Gump" Worsley was born on May 14, 1929, in Montreal, Quebec, Canada. Just as the Great Depression affected so many lives in the United States, it had a similar effect in Canada. Lorne's father, an ironworker by trade, found work hard to find for four years. Of Scottish descent, Lorne was one of three children who grew up in a Montreal suburb of working-class families.

His childhood buddies thought that Lorne resembled a comic book character of that time, Andy Gump, and thus the nickname. As Gump grew up, he no longer resembled the comic character, but the name stuck with him throughout his hockey career. Playing all sports as a youngster, Gump found himself leaning more and more toward goaltending. At first, he was in nets during playground games and later played goalie for the Verdun Cyclones, a Junior League team. It was here that the New York scouts first noticed him and put Lorne on their negotiations list.

The Road to Excellence

For two years, the young Gump played goal for the New York Rovers of the Eastern Amateur League and was also the practice netkeeper for the parent club, the New York Rangers. In 1950, he signed his first professional contract with the St. Paul Saints, where he was the leading goalie in the United States Hockey League. A promotion followed, and Gump played the next season with the Saskatoon Quakers. Finally, during the 1952-53 season, he broke into the big leagues with the New York Rangers and promptly went on to win the Calder Memorial Trophy as the league's outstanding rookie performer. Nothing is assured in the game of professional sports, and Gump was about to learn that. The very next season saw him demoted to the minor leagues. He had a good season there, and the next year he was brought back to the parent club, where he toiled between the pipes for the next ten years.

The New York Rangers was not a good club. In the ten years that Gump played with them, they missed the playoffs six times. When a reporter once asked the always humorous Gump which team gave him the most trouble, he responded that it was the Rangers, his own squad.

The Emerging Champion

At the age of thirty-four, when most athletes are winding down their careers, Gump got a big break. He was traded from the lowly Rangers to the Montreal Canadiens, perennial contenders for the championship. Luck, however, would take time to develop for Gump. After only 8 games, an injury forced him to miss several weeks. When he returned, another hot goalie, Charlie Hodge, had taken his place. He went back to the minors to regain his form. During the next season, Gump was called up when Hodge needed a rest. It was obvious by the second half of the year that the promotion was permanent. In fact, during this season (1964-65) Gump was to play a vital part in Montreal's successful bid for another Stanley Cup.

The following year would be even better, with

2813

Gump and Hodge sharing the honor of winning the Vezina Trophy for the best goaltenders in the game. Also, the Canadiens won the championship again, and Gump was selected to the All-Star team.

Except for his fear of flying, there was very little that could make Gump lose his cool. On the ice, he had a coolness about him that helped him surmount the tensions of every season, even in Montreal, where the pressure to win was great and constant. Even with these growing pressures, Gump's play continued to improve. During the 1967-68 season, he once again made the All-Star Team and repeated as Vezina Trophy winner while his team was clinching yet another league championship. The following year, the Montreal team, with Gump as their main goalie, won the Stanley Cup again.

Continuing the Story

It was during the 1969-70 season, after a particularly bumpy airplane ride, that Gump had enough. He got off the airplane in Toronto and took a train home to Montreal. He announced his retirement the next day. Three months later, after resting and distancing himself from hockey and airplanes, Gump announced his fitness and willingness to return to hockey, this time with the Minnesota North Stars.

He played eight games with this team before the season came to a close, but that was enough of a late surge so that the underdog North Stars made the playoffs. The situation proved so good for Gump that he signed on with Minnesota for the following year. The 1971-72 season was a great one for Gump. He was forty-three years old and playing some of the best hockey of his life. In 1973, age and injuries were catching up with him. Finally, a leg injury slowed him down so much that Gump felt he would be cheating his teammates if he played when he was not completely fit. He retired from active play in January, 1973.

Summary

People who did not know Gump Worsley would see him clowning around or hear him making jokes and would conclude that he was not very serious. They would be mistaken. With a rotund appearance that belied his quickness and a competitive nature that few other players could match, Gump became one of the outstanding goalies ever to play in the National Hockey League.

Carmi Brandis

HONORS AND AWARDS

1953	Calder Memorial Trophy
1966, 1968	Vezina Trophy
1980	Hockey Hall of Fame

STATISTICS

Season	Games	Wins	Losses	Ties	Goals-Against Average	Penalty Minutes
1952-53	50	13	29	8	3.06	2
1954-55	65	15	**33**	17	3.03	2
1955-56	70	32	28	10	2.90	2
1956-57	68	26	28	13	3.24	**19**
1957-58	37	21	10	6	2.32	10
1958-59	67	26	29	12	3.07	10
1959-60	41	8	25	8	3.57	12
1960-61	58	19	**28**	9	3.33	10
1961-62	60	22	**27**	9	2.97	12
1962-63	67	22	**34**	9	3.30	**14**
1963-64	8	3	2	2	2.97	0
1964-65	19	10	7	1	2.78	0
1965-66	51	29	14	6	2.36	4
1966-67	18	9	6	2	3.18	4
1967-68	40	19	9	8	**1.98**	10
1968-69	30	19	6	4	2.25	0
1969-70	14	8	2	3	2.51	0
1970-71	24	4	10	8	2.50	10
1971-72	34	16	10	7	2.12	2
1972-73	12	6	2	3	2.88	22
1973-74	29	8	14	5	3.22	0
Totals	862	335	353	150	2.90	145

NOTE: Boldface indicates statistical leader.

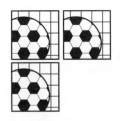

BILLY WRIGHT

Sport: Soccer

Born: February 6, 1924
Ironbridge, England

Early Life

Billy Wright was born on February 6, 1924, in Ironbridge in the English Midlands, 20 miles from Wolverhampton. As a schoolboy he was a fan of the London soccer team Arsenal, who in the 1930's were the leading English team.

Billy always wanted to become a professional soccer player, even though at school he was slightly built and did not excel at the game. However, Norman Simpson, his sports master at Madely Senior School, took note of his potential. In 1937, when Billy was fourteen, Simpson wrote to the famous Wolverhampton Wanderers Football Club (nicknamed the "Wolves") to ask if Wright could be given a job on the ground staff. Billy's father, a worker at the local iron foundry, would have preferred Billy to have joined Aston Villa, another famous Midlands club. Billy's mother, however, was happy with the choice of the Wolves, and as soon as Billy had completed his schooling, he set off for Wolverhampton.

The Road to Excellence

At Wolverhampton, Billy came under the influence of the team manager, Major Frank Buckley, a stern disciplinarian who put him to work doing routine chores. Billy respected Buckley and was bitterly disappointed the next year when Buckley told him he was too small to make the grade as a player and that Buckley was sending him home. Nevertheless, Buckley reversed his decision when the groundsman told him how hard-working and useful Billy was.

By 1939, Billy had played center-forward for the Wolves' "B" team and had made his first-team debut at outside-right. He signed as a professional at the age of seventeen in 1941. After this he settled down as a halfback, the position he was to occupy for the rest of his career.

In the early stages of Billy's career he was indebted to Frank Broome, one of his colleagues on the Wolves team. Broome was a seasoned international forward who taught Billy how to place passes and take up the correct position.

In May, 1942, Billy suffered the worst setback of his career when he broke his ankle during the semifinal of the League War Cup. It was a bad injury, and Buckley and the medical specialists feared it would finish Billy's career—almost before it had begun. Billy remained determined during his recovery, however, and several months later he returned to the Wolves as fit as ever.

The Emerging Champion

In 1947 Billy made his first appearance for England's national team against Belgium at Wembley Stadium in London. Soon he was captaining the Wolves team, and in 1949 he led them to victory in the Football Association Cup final against Leicester City. In the same year he became captain of England.

Billy's game was outstanding for its consistency. He rarely had a bad match. He was fast and had strong tackling ability. Former England manager Ron Greenwood has said that Billy was one of the best ball winners of his era. However, if Billy was beaten in a tackle, he was extremely quick

2817

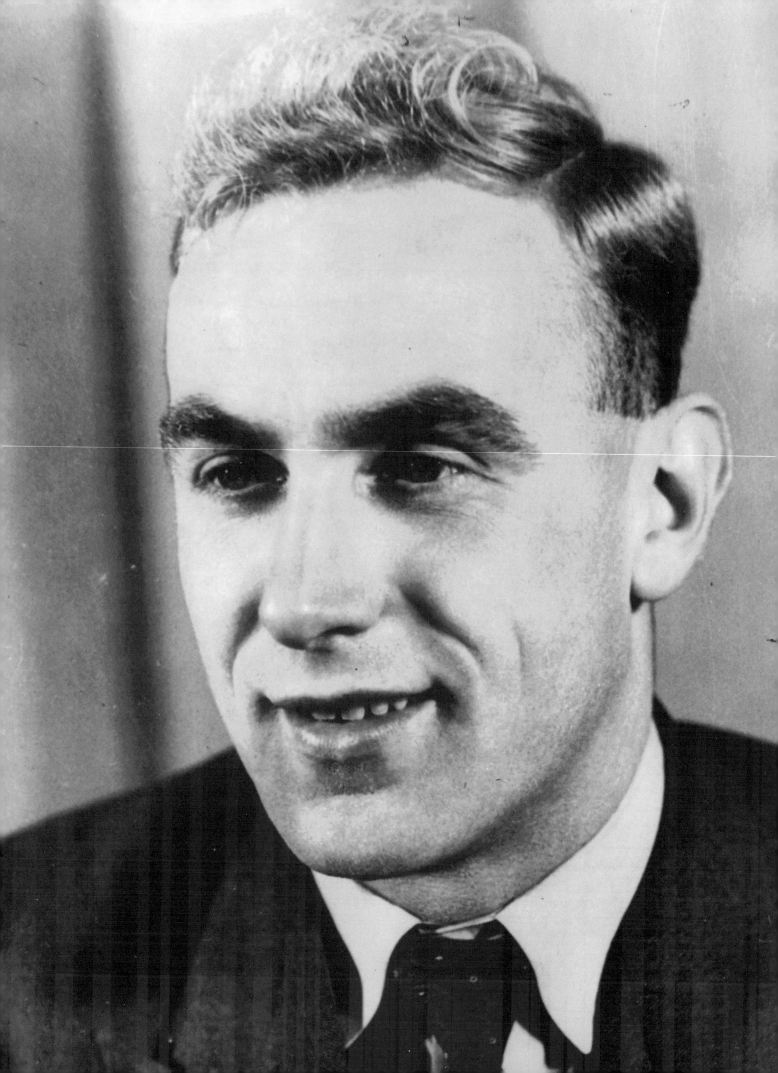

to recover. He was also formidable in the air, since he was usually able to outjump opposing forwards (most of whom were several inches taller than Billy, who stood 5 feet 8 inches).

Billy was a steady and determined player rather than a flamboyant one. He was not an individualist but rather a team player whose style could be integrated easily into that of the rest of the team. He was not known for his forays upfield to support the attack but for solid defensive work. Reluctant to take risks, he put safety first.

As Billy's skills and reputation grew, he learned a great deal from Stan Cullis, who took over from Frank Buckley as the Wolves' manager in 1949. Cullis was a former center-half for the Wolves and for England, and he gave Billy the benefit of his knowledge about tactics and captaincy.

Continuing the Story

In 1952, Billy won the English Footballer of the Year award, and this was a prelude to seven years of almost unbroken success. The Wolves became one of the glamour teams of the 1950's, and Billy captained them to three League championships, in 1954, 1958, and 1959. He also helped the Wolves to some famous victories over some of the best European teams, including Moscow Spartak, Honved of Hungary, and Spain's Real Madrid.

From 1951 to 1959, Billy played 70 consecutive matches for England, a record. He was also the first man to play 100 times for England, most of them as captain. Billy represented England in three World Cup competitions: in Brazil in 1950, Switzerland in 1954, and Sweden in 1958. During the World Cup in 1954, he switched positions from wing-half to center-half, and it is generally thought that this move extended his playing career. Playing in the center of the field meant that he did not have to cover as much ground as he had done at wing-half.

Billy was renowned for his sportsmanship and sense of fair play. He rarely showed anger, and he never argued with a referee over a decision. His loyalty to his club and his country won for him the respect and admiration of the British public. Even when he was well into his thirties, he retained his boyish enthusiasm for the game. Many younger players were thankful to him for his kindness in helping them through their first big matches.

Wright retired from the game in 1959 and was made a Commander of the British Empire (C.B.E.) by Queen Elizabeth II. The award honored his outstanding contribution to English soccer.

For a brief period in the mid-1960's, Wright served as the manager of the Arsenal Football Club in London. He did not achieve the same success as a manager that he had as a player. Some years later, Wright became a successful television executive.

Summary

Billy Wright was one of the finest and most popular players England has produced. An honest and straightforward man, both on the field and off, he was dedicated to his craft. His skill and reliability made him the defensive rock around which the Wolves and England built their teams in the 1950's.

Bryan Aubrey

RECORDS AND MILESTONES

★ 90 times national team captain (world record)
★ 105 international appearances for England

HONORS AND AWARDS

1949	English Football Association Cup champion
1952	English Footballer of the Year
1954, 1958-59	English League champion
1959	Commander of the British Empire

MICKEY WRIGHT

Sport: Golf

Born: February 14, 1935
San Diego, California

Early Life

Mary Kathryn Wright was born in San Diego, California, to attorney Arthur Wright and Mary Kathryn Wright on February 14, 1935. With the same legal name as her mother, she soon became known as "Mickey." Mickey grew into an adolescent with a larger-than-ordinary body. Her friends at school sometimes teased her, calling her "Moose." This teasing gave her an inferiority complex and motivated her to outshine everyone at some skill in order to feel good about herself.

Golf proved to be Mickey's niche. Luckily for her, she was already good at it. Her father was an amateur golfer, and he had encouraged her to practice on a driving range since she was nine years old. By the age of eleven, she played her first round and scored 145. At twelve, she broke 100; at thirteen, she was already down to 80 strokes per round. For years, she had been reading everything she could about golf and keeping scrapbooks of the famous golfers she idolized.

The Road to Excellence

Mickey played in her first tournament in San Diego when she was fifteen. There, she shot a 70. By the next year, she was beating the male professionals at her local course. At one point, her elbow kept flying out too much on the backswing. Professional Paul Runyan showed her how to weaken her grip to fix that. Mickey's mother made her an elastic band that let her arms swing freely but would not allow her elbows to sepa-rate. Mickey practiced by the hour, wearing the contraption. By 1952, she had progressed so well and quickly that she was able to claim victory at the United States Golf Association's Junior Girls' Championship.

Mickey then enrolled in college at Stanford University. When summer came, she was back on the links, proving herself as the best-scoring amateur in the United States Open, as well as the St. Petersburg Open and the Tam O'Shanter tournaments. She was also the runner-up in the United States Amateur. After only one year in college, she convinced her father to let her take a leave of absence from school in order to play as an amateur on the professional tour that coming winter.

Mickey did so well on the tour that, when she calculated what she would have earned had she played as a professional instead of as an amateur, she saw that it made sense for her to immediately switch to professional status.

The Emerging Champion

As a professional, Mickey earned an excellent income right from the start. When she was twenty years old, she earned seven thousand dollars, and then in the next two years, eighty-five hundred dollars and twelve thousand dollars, respectively. By then, 1958, she was winning major tournaments like the Ladies' Professional Golf Association (LPGA) Championship and the United States Open.

Later in that year, though, she went into a slump during the St. Petersburg Open. Her roommate, Betsy Rawls, recognized Mickey's self-pity for what it was and snapped her out of it. Betsy made Mickey see that she could blame her per-

2821

formance on no one but herself.

In 1960, an important year for Mickey, she began to work with her new golf teacher, Earl Stewart, the professional at the Oak Cliff Country Club in Dallas, Texas. She moved to Dallas to be near him. As a first and essential lesson, Stewart taught Mickey how to relax her perfectionistic attitude toward work. He wanted her to play one shot at a time without getting emotionally involved in the shots to come or those behind her. Stewart's primary assistance was psychological, but he also worked on Mickey's swing.

As a result, that same year Mickey won the Vare Trophy for lowest average strokes per round. For the next three years, no one surpassed her average. That was still only the beginning for Mickey. The following year, she achieved a remarkable Grand Slam: She was the winner of the United States Women's Open, the LPGA Championship, and the Titleholders Championship.

It was 1963 that proved to be Mickey's greatest year ever. It was also the greatest year ever achieved by a woman golfer. She won thirteen major tournaments that year, for a lifetime total of fifty-three tournament victories, including her fourth LPGA title. In addition, her average score that year was 72.81, the lowest among all her competitors, for the fourth time. The Associated Press polled sports editors nationwide for their annual selection of Female Athlete of the Year. The choice was easy that year: Mickey Wright.

Continuing the Story

Between 1961 and 1964, Mickey's income surpassed that of all other women golfers. It rose from $18,000 to $31,269. As the finest player in the history of women's golf, she more than deserved it.

In addition to being the best paid, Mickey was also the best long-ball hitter. She surprised many male professionals, who never thought they would see a woman hit the ball 300 yards, by outhitting them on the fairways. Mickey consistently hit drives averaging 225 to 270 yards. Once, aided by a strong wind, she overshot the green of a 385-yard hole. Mickey was a strong, 5-foot 9-inch golfer; she was no longer self-conscious about her size, a trim figure at 150 pounds. Her weaknesses in golf changed, she found. When a weakness was evident in her swing, she practiced and analyzed her swing in front of a mirror. At other times, she was considered weak on the greens in the short game—shots from 130 to 140 yards onto the green.

Her swing was considered the best of all time. Golfers everywhere marveled at her grace and balance and at how well her swing was synchronized. She never appeared to be swinging hard, yet she could hit as far as the men professionals. She was the Jack Nicklaus of women's driving, with the best combination of distance and distance on the fly.

Later on, Mickey went into the brokerage business, while living in Port St. Lucie, Florida. When she injured her back, she stopped playing golf regularly.

Summary

Mickey Wright was the greatest long-ball hitter in the history of women's golf. She is often considered the finest woman golfer ever. She won both the LPGA title and the United States Women's Open four times and the Vare Trophy four years in a row. For two years in succession, she was named Female Athlete of the Year by the Associated Press. She was the first woman ever to win as many as thirteen major tournaments in a single year. For these achievements, she was inducted to the LPGA Hall of Fame.

Nan White

MAJOR CHAMPIONSHIP VICTORIES

1958-59, 1961, 1964	U.S. Women's Open
1958, 1960-61, 1963	LPGA Championship
1961-62	Titleholders Championship
1962-63, 1966	Western Open
1973	Colgate Dinah Shore

OTHER NOTABLE VICTORIES

1960	Eastern Open
1960	Memphis Open
1961, 1963, 1966	Mickey Wright Invitational
1961, 1963	St. Petersburg Open
1963	Babe Zaharias Open
1966-67, 1969	Bluegrass Invitational
1967	Baltimore Lady Carling
1967	Pensacola Invitational

RECORDS AND MILESTONES

★ Eighty-two career victories
★ Won a record thirteen victories in 1963
★ Tour's leading money winner four times (1961-64)
★ Had at least one tournament victory a year (1956-70)
★ Only woman golfer to win the U.S. Women's Open and the LPGA Championship in the same year twice (1958, 1961)
★ Her collection of four U.S. Women's Open titles is a record shared with Betsy Rawls

HONORS AND AWARDS

1957	*Golf Digest* Most Improved Golfer
1958, 1960-64	*Golf Digest* Mickey Wright Award for Tournament Victories
1958-67	*Golf* Magazine Golfer of the Decade
1960-64	LPGA Vare Trophy
1963-64	Associated Press Female Athlete of the Year
1964	LPGA Hall of Fame
1976	PGA/World Golf Hall of Fame
1981	Sudafed International Women's Sports Hall of Fame

EARLY WYNN

Sport: Baseball

Born: January 6, 1920
Hartford, Alabama

Early Life

Early Wynn was born on January 6, 1920, in Hartford, Alabama, a village in southeastern Alabama where his father, a semiprofessional baseball player, worked as an auto mechanic. A fine athlete as a young boy, Early always could throw hard and seemed destined to pitch, as he did for the Hartford baseball team. He was also an excellent halfback for the high school football team, but this ended soon because, midway through high school, he broke his leg just before football season. As a result, in the following spring, baseball became his only sport. He quit school during that spring, attended a baseball training camp in Sanford, Florida, and was offered a one-hundred-dollar-a-month contract by a scout from the Washington Senators. Even though he had intended to return to high school, this was too tempting an offer for a boy who had spent the previous summer working on a cotton gin.

The Road to Excellence

Early's first season was spent on the Sanford team in the Florida State League, where he earned 16 victories in 235 innings. The next years brought tragedy, however. While playing for the Charlotte, North Carolina, team in 1939, Early married Mabel Allman. Two years later, after the birth of a son, Joe Early, he lost her in an automobile accident as she drove home a baby-sitter.

The pain of this event and the responsibility of a baby son caused Early to work at his career with more earnestness. As a result, he was called up to the Washington Senators in 1940. In 1943, he earned 18 wins, but the following year brought only an 8-17 season. With World War II still raging, Early enlisted in the Army. During the same year, he married Lorraine Follin. By 1946, he had returned to pitching for the Senators, but the failing Senators team, combined with Early's one-pitch repertoire (fastball), brought three lacklustre seasons. Early was traded to Bill Veeck's Cleveland Indians along with Micky Vernon at the end of 1948 for Joe Haynes, Ed Klieman, and Eddie Robinson. This stands as one of the most beneficial trades in the history of the Cleveland Indians.

The Emerging Champion

The trade was beneficial to Early Wynn's career also. He began to work under the tutelage of coach Mel Harder, who helped Early to control a curveball, a knuckleball, a slider, and a change-up. With such variety and skill, Early was able to achieve 163 wins and four 20-game seasons during his nine-year stay with the Indians. Besides this, he served in one of the greatest rotations in baseball history: Early, Bob Lemon, Mike Garcia, and Bob Feller, replaced by Herb Score. They brought the team to second place in 1952 and 1953 when Garcia, Lemon, and Wynn were named Cleveland Men of the Year. They guided the team to the pennant in 1954, one of only two seasons when the New York Yankees did not take it during their stellar 1950's decade.

Nearing the age of thirty-eight, Early Wynn, along with Al Smith, was traded to the fast-

2825

moving, weak-hitting Chicago White Sox for Minnie Minoso and Fred Hatfield. They were intended to help the Chicago team's chances for an American League pennant, and help they did. In the 1959 season, Early pitched a 22-win season, which helped to cinch the American League pennant. He won the Cy Young Award and continued to a 13-win season at the age of forty in 1960.

Continuing the Story

With 284 career wins, Early was only 16 games from the magic 300-win career, but at the end of a 7-15 season in 1962, the gout-plagued Wynn was released by the White Sox with 299 wins.

His old team, the Cleveland Indians, offered him a year's contract, which gave him an opportunity to earn that one final victory. On July 13, after three failed attempts, Wynn pitched five innings against Kansas City, leaving the mound with a score of 5-4, and the Indians enforced the win 7-4. Early became the fourteenth pitcher in history to win 300 games.

While continuing to pitch for the remainder of the season, Early never earned another victory. He coached for the Indians for three years and then for the Minnesota Twins for three years, where, in 1969, he was named a super scout. He was inducted into the National Baseball Hall of Fame in 1972.

Summary

A hard loser, known for his toughness, Early Wynn joked that he would knock down his grandmother if she dug in against him. He enjoyed 300 wins in a twenty-three-year career, the longest in the major leagues to that time. Such longevity and enormous success are indeed rare among pitchers.

Vicki K. Robinson

HONORS AND AWARDS

1955-60	American League All-Star Team
1959	Cy Young Award
1959	*The Sporting News* Major League Player of the Year
1972	National Baseball Hall of Fame

STATISTICS

Season	Games	Games Started	Games Completed	Innings Pitched	Hits Allowed	Walks	Strikeouts	Wins	Losses	Saves	Shutouts	ERA
1939	3	3	1	20.1	26	10	1	0	2	0	0	5.75
1941	5	5	4	40	35	10	15	3	1	0	0	1.58
1942	30	28	10	190	246	73	58	10	16	0	1	5.12
1943	37	33	12	256.2	232	83	89	18	12	0	3	2.91
1944	33	25	19	207.2	221	67	65	8	17	2	2	3.38
1946	17	12	9	107	112	33	36	8	5	0	0	3.11
1947	33	31	22	247	251	90	73	17	15	0	2	3.64
1948	33	31	15	198	236	94	49	8	19	0	1	5.82
1949	26	23	6	164.2	186	57	62	11	7	0	0	4.15
1950	32	28	14	213.2	166	101	143	18	8	0	2	**3.20**
1951	37	34	21	274.1	227	107	133	20	13	1	3	3.02
1952	42	33	19	285.2	239	132	153	23	12	3	4	2.90
1953	36	34	16	251.2	234	107	138	17	12	0	1	3.93
1954	40	36	20	270.2	225	83	155	**23**	11	2	3	2.73
1955	32	31	16	230	207	80	122	17	11	0	6	2.82
1956	38	35	18	277.2	233	91	158	20	9	2	4	2.72
1957	40	37	13	263	270	104	**184**	14	17	1	1	4.31
1958	40	34	11	239.2	214	104	**179**	14	16	2	4	4.13
1959	37	37	14	255.2	202	119	179	**22**	10	0	5	3.17
1960	36	35	13	237.1	220	112	158	13	12	1	**4**	3.49
1961	17	16	5	110.1	88	47	64	8	2	0	0	3.51
1962	27	26	11	167.2	171	56	91	7	15	0	3	4.46
1963	20	5	1	55.1	50	15	29	1	2	1	0	2.28
Totals	691	612	290	4,564	4,291	1,775	2,334	300	244	15	49	3.54

NOTE: Boldface indicates statistical leader.

YASUHIRO YAMASHITA

Sport: Judo

Born: 1958
Yabe, Kyushu, Japan

Early Life

Yasuhiro Yamashita was born in 1958 in a farming village of sixteen thousand people in the Miharashi-Dai hills of Yabe, Kyushu, Japan. Yasuhiro's grandfather had previously lost two of his own children, and he did not want to lose his grandson Yasuhiro, so he made sure that Yasuhiro was properly taken care of and well fed. Therefore, at the age of one, Yasuhiro won a local contest as the healthiest baby. When Yasuhiro was in elementary school, he was full of energy and determination; he was not satisfied until he became the best at everything he tried, and he was not afraid to fight older and even bigger boys to protect his smaller and weaker friends. He was very strong but kind and fair.

He first became interested in judo at age ten, when his mother took him to a local dojo (martial arts school) because she wanted him to gain control over his aggression. Yamashita loved judo. He could now trip and fling other children and get smiles from his teachers instead of angry looks. One day, Reisuke Shiraishi, who was a sensei (martial arts master) at a distant Kumamoto junior high school, saw Yasuhiro compete in a judo tournament. Shiraishi asked Yasuhiro to move to Kumamoto and vowed to make him a champion. Yasuhiro felt the Japanese traditional loyalty to his family, friends, and school, and he said no. One night, however, his father and younger brother took Yasuhiro to Kumamoto while he was asleep. The sensei gave Yasuhiro a white uniform and asked him to practice with the other students. The well-trained students tossed Yasuhiro left and right because he had not been trained as well. That day, Yasuhiro discovered that he hated losing more than moving to Kumamoto, so he moved to Kumamoto to study judo.

The Road to Excellence

On school days, Yasuhiro practiced from 4:30 to 8:00 P.M. When there was no school, he practiced ten hours a day. The first thing the sensei did was change Yasuhiro from being right-handed to being left-handed, which made him a more difficult opponent. During a single year, he gained 55 pounds and began to progress toward the heavyweight division at judo competitions. Yasuhiro was taught to see each opponent as a man who had just slain his parents, to bow to him with respect, and then to attack without mercy.

One day, a sensei from Tokai University, an institution famous for martial arts, asked Yasuhiro to finish his last two years at their feeder school (a school universities use to prepare future students), because the competition would be more fierce than at Yasuhiro's traditional school. At first, Yasuhiro declined, but when he lost in the semifinals of the national high school championships, defeat made him once more remember that he hated losing more than moving, and he left right away.

When Yasuhiro went to Tokai University, he began training with Radomir Kovacevic, a young martial arts student from Yugoslavia. They would train with Kovacevic riding piggyback up hills on Yasuhiro's back to build Yasuhiro's strength. Be-

2829

cause he was working with someone stronger and heavier, Yasuhiro soon turned his body fat to muscle, and his stamina improved. As a result of his training, at the age of nineteen, Yasuhiro became the youngest man to win the All-Japan Judo Championships (the Japanese equivalent to football's Heisman Trophy).

The Emerging Champion

Because Yasuhiro was so good, Dr. Shigeyoshi Matsumae, President of the International Judo Federation, used him as a judo leader and coach. Matsumae sent Yasuhiro to many countries to encourage foreigners to come and train under him at Tokai University and to promote friendship and world peace. No one else had ever had such a significant judo position in Japan's recent history.

In October, 1977, Yasuhiro was jolted. In the final of the Japan Student Championships, he hesitated, believing the match was over. Because of his hesitation, the judges awarded the decision to his rival. This setback helped Yasuhiro to remain consistently aggressive throughout his matches. He then became an undefeated champion and began to prepare himself for the 1980 Olympics.

In 1980, however, before a national television audience and members of the Japan Amateur Sports Federation, Yasuhiro stood weeping and pleading that the Sports Federation not devastate his dream of going to the 1980 Moscow Olympics because of the international boycott. A week later, he walked onto the mat to face another judo champion, Sumio Endo. Because of his disappointment about the Olympics, Yasuhiro was not able to concentrate and, during the match, Endo used a questionable throw that broke Yasuhiro's ankle. Yasuhiro's long recovery heightened his desire to win.

Not long after, the promoters of Japanese Professional Wrestling (sumo wrestling) paid Yasuhiro's grandfather the equivalent of $45,000 to help them recruit his grandson as a professional athlete. If Yasuhiro agreed, the grandfather would receive another $250,000. Yasuhiro, however,

wanted to maintain his amateur standing in judo. He told his grandfather to return the money and never to talk to the professional wrestling committee again or his relationship with his grandfather was over.

Yasuhiro lived a simple life in a small home crammed with gifts and trinkets given to him by friends. He continued to compete, earning 194 consecutive wins. Finally, in 1984, Yasuhiro captured the Olympic gold medal in judo by winning the open-weights event (no weight restrictions on his 5-foot 10-inch, 280-pound body) during the Summer Olympics in Los Angeles. He finally had won the medal of his dreams. The twenty-six-year-old Tokai University judo coach had now won all the major judo awards possible. His Olympic victory confirmed his reputation as the undisputed world judo champion.

Continuing the Story

Yasuhiro became a Japanese hero, a great example of true sportsmanship because he did not sell out to money. Many Japanese children long to be like him. Yasuhiro gained strength day by day and year by year through hard training, but he never forgot his spirit. He could make significant amounts of money because of his fame, but he says, "Of course I need money, but even more, I want to push my chest out and lift my head and work proudly." He would maintain a simple life, spending his time training future judo athletes and endorsing various products.

Yasuhiro would continue to help Dr. Matsumae's dream come true to use judo to promote world peace. His personality as well as his fame would help to accomplish this dream. He is open to everyone, humble, and gentle, despite his huge body.

Summary

No one has been able to equal Yasuhiro Yamashita's accomplishments in judo. He has won more awards and titles than anyone else in the sport, including four-time World Judo Champion,

Yasuhiro Yamashita, left, grapples with long-time rival Hitoshi Saito.

nine-time All-Japan Judo Champion, and a judo gold medal in the 1984 Olympics. He would be an influential master sensei of martial arts at To- kai University and would maintain his gentle personality despite his formidable size.

Rodney D. Keller

MAJOR CHAMPIONSHIPS

Year	Competition	Weight Class	Place
1977-85	All-Japan Judo Championships	—	1st
1977-79	All-Japan Weight-Class Championships	Open-weights	1st
1978, 1982	Jigoro Kano Cup International Championships	Open-weights	1st
1978	Jigoro Kano Cup International Championships	Heavyweight	1st
1979, 1981, 1983	World Judo Championships	+95kg	Gold
1979	Paris International	+95kg	1st
1980, 1982-83	All-Japan Weight-Class Championships	+95kg	1st
1981	World Judo Championships	Open-weights	Gold
1984	Olympic Games	Open-weights	Gold

CALE YARBOROUGH

Sport: Auto racing

Born: March 27, 1939
Timmonsville, South Carolina

Early Life

William Caleb Yarborough was born on March 27, 1939, in Timmonsville, South Carolina. He grew up on his parent's tobacco farm in Sardis, South Carolina, a small rural community of little more than 150 people. Cale had a happy home life and loved to play and explore on the family farm. Even as a very young boy, Cale was used to being at the wheel of a car or truck. He would often sit on the lap of one of his father's farm workers as they drove errands in the pickup. By the age of eight, he was driving around the farm on his own.

Cale's first taste of driving competition came in 1950, when he entered a local soapbox race. Cale spent hours preparing his racer and looked forward to competing against other children. In the end, Cale did not win the race. Losing was a terrible feeling, and from this moment on, Cale decided that he wanted to be a winner. This competitive edge, which Cale acquired so young, was ultimately to enable him to become one of the greatest stock car racers of all time.

The Road to Excellence

From an early age, Cale loved anything having to do with cars and driving, but he was also an outstanding all-around athlete while attending Timmonsville High School. Cale won the South Carolina Golden Gloves welterweight boxing title and he was also an All-State running back. Clearly, Cale had many athletic talents and it was by no means certain that he would end up in auto racing.

At one stage, it appeared that Cale was headed for a career in professional football. After attending Clemson University on a football scholarship for a short while, Cale played semiprofessional football for the Sumter, South Carolina, Generals. He was even offered a tryout with the Washington Redskins. Cale declined the offer and once and for all decided that he was going to make a career in his first love—auto racing.

By the age of seventeen, Cale was an accomplished stock car driver, having won the South Carolina Stock Car Sportsman Championship. This level of racing allowed Cale to make enough money to support himself and his new bride, but he had a burning ambition to get to the top of the sport.

To make it big in stock car racing, Cale knew he would have to be successful on the highly competitive Grand National Circuit of the National Association for Stock Car Auto Racing (NASCAR). For a long time, NASCAR success eluded Cale; he went seven years on the circuit without a win. Finally, in 1965, Cale secured his first victory, and in that season, he went on to finish in the top ten in thirty-four races. He also amassed $25,140 in prize money. After years of patient learning, Cale had arrived on the NASCAR circuit.

The Emerging Champion

Between 1965 and 1970, Cale won fourteen NASCAR championship races. His big year came in 1968, however, when he won six NASCAR races and $136,786 in prize money. Probably his

2833

most satisfying victory of the 1968 season came in the Southern 500, held in Darlington, South Carolina, near his home. In a grueling race, Cale eventually outlasted David Pearson to record an emotional victory on the track he had frequented as a child.

Having come to dominate the NASCAR circuit, Cale became restless and looked for a new challenge. To this end, in the early 1970's, Cale tried his hand at single-seater racing on the USAC circuit. Although not a total failure, Cale found it difficult to adjust to this form of competition. After two frustrating seasons, he returned to stock car racing.

In 1973, Cale returned to the NASCAR circuit with great enthusiasm, and in the following two years he won a total of seventeen NASCAR races. The aggressive driving and fierce will to win, which hampered his performances in single-seater racing, once again made him a dominating force in stock car competition.

Cale was reaching his peak as an auto racer and was about to embark upon the most successful phase of his career. Between 1976 and 1978, Cale dominated the stock car scene like no one else before him. In these three seasons, Cale won twenty-eight NASCAR races and won the Winston Cup (the NASCAR circuit driving title) three times. These triumphs earned him nearly $1.5 million in prize money.

Continuing the Story

Following his three-year domination of the stock car world, Cale gradually concentrated less and less on racing. Between 1979 and his retirement in 1986, he competed in an average of only sixteen races a year.

Despite his relative inactivity, Cale was still successful, winning twenty-four more races, to bring his career total to eighty-eight NASCAR victories. As of 1991, this figure ranks him fourth on the all-time list behind Richard Petty, David Pearson, and Bobby Allison. Cale's victory at the Southern 500 in 1982 gave him an unprecedented fifth triumph in that race. It is perhaps fitting that Cale should so dominate the race held in his own "backyard."

Throughout his racing career, Cale displayed a single-minded confidence in his own ability and a fierce competitive spirit. These attributes enabled him to amass $5,003,616 in prize money by the time of his retirement in 1986. Cale invested his earnings wisely and would manage his numerous thriving business interests with the same drive and determination that characterized his racing career.

Summary

Cale Yarborough always believed in his ability to make it to the top as a stock car driver. He kept this self-confidence even through the long, unsuccessful learning phase of his career. As a result of his patience and perseverance, Cale ultimately realized his dream, becoming one of the best stock car racers the sport has ever seen.

David L. Andrews

HONORS, AWARDS, AND RECORDS

1967	NASCAR Winston Cup Most Popular Driver
1968	Ford Motor Company Man of the Year
1968-69, 1978-79	Union 76-Darlington Record Club
1977	Olsonite Driver of the Year
1978	Only driver to win three consecutive NASCAR Winston Cup Championships
1982	Only driver to win the Southern 500 five times
1991	American Auto Racing Writers and Broadcasters Association Hall of Fame

NASCAR AND OTHER VICTORIES

Year	Event
1957	South Carolina Stock Car Sportsman Championship
1967-69, 1974, 1981, 1983	Coca-Cola 500
1967-68, 1976, 1981	Pepsi 400
1968, 1973-74, 1978, 1982	Southern 500
1968, 1977, 1983-84	Daytona 500
1968, 1974, 1977	Virginia 500
1969	Miller Genuine Draft 500
1970, 1974, 1977, 1982, 1984-85	Daytona 500 Twin 125 Qualifying Race
1970, 1977	Miller Genuine Draft 400
1970, 1975, 1978, 1980	Nationwide 500
1973-74, 1976-77	Valleydale Meats 500
1973, 1979	National 500
1973, 1976, 1978-79	Music City 420
1974, 1976-78, 1980	Busch 500
1974	Riverside 400
1974, 1977	Mason-Dixon 500
1974-75	Nashville 420
1974, 1976, 1978	Wilkes 400
1975, 1980, 1982	Carolina 500
1976	Delaware 500
1976-77	Staley 400
1976-78	Old Dominion 500
1976	Capital City 400
1976-78	NASCAR Winston Cup Champion
1977, 1979	Richmond 400
1978, 1984	Winston 500
1978, 1982-83	Gabriel 400
1979	Mountain Dew 500
1980, 1983	Champion Spark Plug 400
1980	Texas 400
1980	Atlanta Journal 500
1984	International Race of Champions
1984	Van Scoy Diamond Mines 500
1985	Miller High Life 500
1985	Talladega 500
1986	Budweiser International Race of Champions, third-round winner

IVAN YARYGIN

Sport: Wrestling

Born: November 7, 1948
        Vst'-Kamzas, Siberia,
          the Soviet Union

Early Life

Ivan Yarygin was born on November 7, 1948, in Vst'-Kamzas, Siberia, the Soviet Union. He was the seventh child in a family where children were expected to help with chores such as cutting grass for the cattle, chopping wood, and working in the blacksmith's shop. His family eventually settled in Sizaya, Siberia.

Ivan attended a school three kilometers from his home. In the summer, he covered the distance by running or biking, and in the winter, on cross-country skis. By the age of fifteen, he was of exceptional size and strength. He stayed late after school to play his favorite sport, soccer. He played goalie, and it seemed to be impossible to score a goal against him.

After completing school, Ivan went to Abakan to attend a training school for truck drivers. He also played on the school's soccer team. It was at one of these games that the coach of the local wrestling school, Vladimir Charkov, saw him and thought that this big strapping man would be a natural on the wrestling mat. He would eventually grow to 6 feet 4 inches and 220 pounds.

The Road to Excellence

It took a while for Charkov to overcome Ivan's great love for soccer. Through his persistence, he finally induced Ivan to attend a wrestling school. At an early meet, Ivan took last place because of a lack of technical skills, became discouraged, and

returned to his hometown without saying goodbye.

Charkov tracked him down, going first to his home, and then driving a motorboat 170 kilometers up a river to a remote point in the Russian taiga, where Ivan and his father had gone for logging. Ivan's father, despite some misgivings, did not stand in the way, and Ivan agreed to return to Abakan. After three months of intensive training, Ivan went to Krasnoyarsk for a meet. It was there that coach Dmitry G. Mindiashvili of the Krasnoyarsk wrestling school saw him for the first time and immediately thought that he would go far.

After a few more wrestling meets, Ivan moved to Krasnoyarsk to be coached by Mindiashvili at Charkov's suggestion. He lived at the coach's house and held down a job as a metal worker at a tire factory. Ivan's training was interrupted by the required term of military service in which, based on his athletic promise, he was assigned to a company for athletes. He also married Natasha, and a daughter, Annuska, was born in 1971, and a son, Sergei, in 1973.

The Emerging Champion

As the 1972 Munich Olympics approached, Ivan was selected for the freestyle team and began to achieve great success at major national and international meets. Ivan won the gold medal (100 kg weight division) at the 1972 Olympics held in Munich, Germany. The Mongolian, Hollogin Baianmunh, finished second and Josef Csatari of Hungary finished third. At the 1973 World Cup in Toledo, Ohio, Ivan again won the gold medal with Josef Csatari finishing second and Demitar Nekov of Bulgaria, third.

2837

A slump, beginning in 1974 and continuing through 1975, cast doubts on Ivan's wrestling career as well as his possibility of making the 1976 Olympic team. He fell ill at the 1974 European Championships in Madrid, losing to the East German, Harold Buttner, in the final. He could not shake his sickness and finished fifth in the Nationals at Uf. After recovering but still only taking third at the Spartacade of Soviet People in Kiev in 1975, he thought of retiring, but renewed his mind and body as he had done at other critical parts of his life by spending time in the wilderness. This time he spent a whole month hunting in the dense forests of the Russian taiga.

Ivan regained his form for the 1976 World Cup in Toledo, winning all his matches. He then emerged from the European Championships in Leningrad with a ferocious new vigor. At the Montreal, Canada, Olympics, in 1976, he ironically drew Harold Buttner, the rival to whom he had lost not just once, but twice, for his first match. He defeated Buttner and went on to win the gold medal. Russ Hellickson of the United States finished second and Demo Kostov of Bulgaria, third.

Continuing the Story

Ivan became a champion in spite of the fact that he started wrestling at the rather advanced age of seventeen. Ivan continued training for the 1980 Moscow Olympics. He made a final massive personal effort in 1979, but to his great disappointment, failed to make the team. The next generation of gold medal winners was already beginning to take over.

In 1980, Ivan became the Soviet national team coach at thirty-three years old. In the course of the 1980's, his wrestlers achieved great success despite the ever-increasing quality of the international competition. It was not unusual for every one of Ivan's wrestlers to win a medal at the various World Championships. The majority would usually win gold medals.

Ivan has made Krasnoyarsk his hometown. A new wrestling tournament is now held annually in Krasnoyarsk in Ivan's honor, called the Yarygin International.

Summary

Ivan Yarygin was a great two-time Olympic wrestling champion and an outstanding Soviet national wrestling team coach. Twice during his wrestling career, Ivan conquered a loss of self-confidence resulting from wrestling defeats to become a champion. During the 1980's, his wrestlers dominated the various World Wrestling Championships.

Carl F. Rothfuss
Walter R. Schneider

MAJOR CHAMPIONSHIPS

Year	Competition	Weight Class	Place
1972	Olympic Games	100kg	Gold
1973	World Championships	100kg	Gold
1973	World Cup	100kg	Gold
1976	Olympic Games	100kg	Gold
1976	World Cup	100kg	Gold

INTERNATIONAL COACHING RECORD

Year	Competition	Team Place
1982	World Championships	1st
1983	World Championships	1st
1985	World Championships	1st
1986	Goodwill Games	1st
1986	World Championships	1st
1987	World Championships	1st
1988	Olympic Games	1st
1989	World Championships	1st
1990	Goodwill Games	2d
1990	World Championships	1st
1991	World Championships	1st

2840

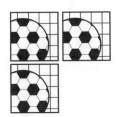

LEV YASHIN

Born: October 22, 1929
      Moscow, Soviet Union
Died: March 21, 1990
      Moscow, Soviet Union

Early Life

Lev Ivanovich Yashin was born in Moscow, the capital of Russia and of the Soviet Union, on October 22, 1929. His parents were factory workers, and the family lived in an older-style wooden communal apartment building on the outskirts of the city.

When Lev was a boy during the 1930's, life in Moscow was difficult. Most people were poor, and many were persecuted by the Soviet government. One of the few pleasant distractions from such concerns was participation in sports. As a boy, Lev began his sports career by playing hockey with friends on a frozen pond near his home. From an early age, he earned a reputation as an uncanny keeper of the goal. Working with very limited equipment—often no mask, no body padding, and no glove—Lev would do whatever he had to do to stop the puck from getting past him. He was of ordinary size, but with long legs and arms, and he was extremely wiry and quick. Because it seemed that he could always get an arm out to intercept any shot at the goal, his friends began to call him "Octopus."

The Road to Excellence

The distractive powers of sport proved even more important in Lev's life during World War II. In late 1941, Nazi armies had almost reached Moscow. They were repelled only by the most con-

certed effort, involving not only the military, in which Lev was still too young to serve, but the civilian population of the city as well. Lev's parents were heroically engaged in the effort. Lev himself spent all his nonschool time playing on hockey teams sponsored by the Communist Youth Organization in order to entertain the struggling populace. In the summer, Lev and his friends would turn their athletic skills to soccer, the sport in which he was to achieve lasting renown. By the time the war ended, Lev had become one of the most highly regarded goalkeepers in the Moscow youth leagues.

When Lev finished high school in 1946, he went to work in the factories, as his parents had before him. He stayed active in soccer, however, by playing with a number of Moscow soccer clubs. He then played on a Soviet army team while completing his two-year military service obligation. Returning to civilian life in 1950, Lev was accepted as a backup goalkeeper for one of Moscow's most popular world-class soccer teams, Dynamo. The remainder of Lev's career was associated with this great team.

In 1954, Dynamo's regular goalkeeper became ill, and Lev was called upon to play in important games. His performance assured his permanence in the position. His athletic dives to stop opposing kicks thrilled the huge crowds that attended Dynamo's games with teams from other cities and with Moscow rivals Torpedo and Spartak. In the next two years, no team scored more than two goals against Lev's defense, and Dynamo was the national champion in 1954 and again in 1955. Lev's popularity soared as did his standard of living in

Soviet society. He was chosen to represent his country in the 1956 Olympic Games in Melbourne, Australia, and thanks largely to his sparkling defense, his team was victorious.

The Emerging Champion

In 1956, Soviet Premier Nikita Khrushchev initiated a thaw in the restrictions on art, dance, music, and literature, a development that occasioned much hope among the Soviet people. With such a spirit of hope, Lev Yashin became a member of the Communist Party in 1957. It is also possible that Party membership played a part in his selection for the Soviet Union's World Cup team in 1958 and for the Soviet team that won the first European Championship in 1960. Lev's play in these tournaments was extraordinary, establishing him internationally as soccer's leading goalkeeper.

In the remaining years of the 1960's, Lev was active on two more Soviet Olympic teams (1960 in Rome and 1964 in Tokyo) and on two more World Cup teams. With the exception of a disconcertingly mediocre series of games in South America during the 1962 World Cup competition, Lev was continually remarkable in defense of the goal. Soccer analysts attributed his success to his amazingly quick reactions and his fine sense of anticipation of the action, but Lev himself often said he was simply willing to sacrifice more of himself physically than others were in order to stop the ball.

Yet despite such apparent sacrifice, Lev was rarely injured. Perhaps his luck can be attributed to his schedule of almost constant play: daily practice, weekly games with Dynamo, and a record 78 games with the Soviet national team. In 1963, he was the first goalkeeper named European Player of the Year and received soccer's coveted Ballon d'Or Award.

Continuing the Story

As he approached forty years of age, Lev gradually began to take more of a coaching rather than a playing role with Dynamo. He also served as adviser to the Soviet national team. In 1972, he announced his official retirement as a soccer player. In that year also he was graduated from the prestigious Moscow Higher Party School, a leadership training institution of the Communist Party's Central Committee. He then became an administrator of the Dynamo team and a member of the Soviet Union's State Council on Physical Culture and Sports. In his eighteen years in this capacity, he was central in the Soviet Union's eventual formal recognition of the professional status of its athletes. Before his death of stomach cancer on March 21, 1990, he approved a measure to give state pensions to world-class athletes whose competitive youth deprived them of other life skills in a society that gave them little reward except renown.

In June of 1990, two months after Lev's death in Moscow, the yearly Lev Yashin Invitational Soccer Tournament was instituted in his honor in Anchorage, Alaska.

Summary

Lev Yashin's remarkable saves as a soccer goalie helped change the popular view of that position from that of a peripheral function to one of central importance to a team's success. Fans of soccer all over the world still recognize a "Yashin style" of play for goalkeepers. After his days as a player were over, Lev continued to devote his life to the advancement of sport.

Lee B. Croft

HONORS AND AWARDS

1954-55, 1957, 1959, 1963	Soviet League champion
1956	Olympic Gold Medal
1960	European Championship champion
1960, 1965-66	Soviet Goalkeeper of the Year
1963	European Player of the Year (Ballon d'Or)

MILESTONES

★ 78 international appearances for the Soviet Union

CARL YASTRZEMSKI

Sport: Baseball

Born: August 22, 1939
Southampton, New York

Early Life

Carl Michael Yastrzemski was born on August 22, 1939, in Southampton, New York, the son of Hedwig and Carl Yastrzemski. He grew up in the small Long Island town of Bridgehampton, a Polish community of potato farmers. His parents' families, the Skoniecznys and the Yastrzemskis, worked the potato fields together.

Although his parents expected him to contribute to the family farm, Carl practiced his hitting and pitching almost every day from the age of six. His family encouraged his early interest in the sport; indeed, his father was a talented player who had to pass up an opportunity to sign minor league contracts with the Brooklyn Dodgers and the St. Louis Cardinals because they offered so little money. Instead, Carl's father managed and played on a local team, the Bridgehampton White Eagles. Carl got his first taste of organized baseball when he became the team's batboy.

The Road to Excellence

Carl was the best player at all the levels of baseball he attempted, in Little League, Babe Ruth baseball, and high school and semiprofessional teams. At fifteen, he joined his father on the White Eagles. While his father played second base and batted fourth, Carl played shortstop and batted third. Throughout his early playing days, Carl's father remained the major influence in his life as a teacher and an inspiration to do his best.

Carl was not only an outstanding hitter and pitcher but also a talented basketball player. After considering several offers, Carl accepted a scholarship to play baseball and basketball at the University of Notre Dame in 1957.

Following a disappointing year when he was not permitted to train with the varsity teams, Carl signed a professional contract with the Boston Red Sox. He had tryouts and offers from many teams, including the Detroit Tigers, the Los Angeles Dodgers, the Philadelphia Phillies, and his childhood favorite, the New York Yankees. His father, however, believed Carl would have greater success hitting at Boston's Fenway Park, so the nineteen-year-old became a member of the Red Sox in 1958.

Carl enjoyed two spectacular years in the minor leagues. In 1959 at Raleigh, North Carolina, he batted a Carolina League-leading .377. The following season, Carl barely missed winning the International League batting title with Minneapolis, hitting .339.

The Emerging Champion

In 1960, Boston all-time great Ted Williams retired, and the Red Sox decided that Carl was ready to replace him in left field. His rookie season in 1961, however, was difficult. Fans and reporters expected him to replace a baseball legend, and he felt pressured to succeed immediately. Despite the difficulties, Carl batted a strong .266 and established himself as a master in handling balls hit off the famous "Green Monster" left field fence in Fenway Park.

Although he continued to improve as a hitter and won the American League batting title in

2845

1963, Carl and Boston fans remained disappointed with the team's repeated failures. During his first six seasons, the team never finished higher than sixth in the standings. Determined to improve himself and the team, Carl spent the winter after the 1966 season working with Hungarian Olympic coach Gene Berde.

Joining the trimmer, stronger Yastrzemski on the 1967 Red Sox were emerging stars Jim Lonborg, George Scott, Reggie Smith, and Tony Conigliaro. They became the "Impossible Dream" team for Boston fans. Baseball experts picked them to finish ninth, but the Red Sox won the American League pennant on the last day of the season. Carl, as he would do throughout his career in tough situations, was almost perfect at the plate in the last two games. He had base hits in his last six at-bats.

The Red Sox could not complete the "Dream." They lost the World Series to the St. Louis Cardinals in seven games. The loss did nothing to diminish the significance of Carl's year. He became the last player in either league to win the Triple Crown. Carl led the league in batting with a .326 average, in home runs with 44, and in runs batted in with 121. The baseball writers named him the league's Most Valuable Player, *Sports Illustrated* named him Sportsman of the Year, and the Associated Press chose him as Male Athlete of the Year.

Continuing the Story

Carl would have other great seasons. In 1970, he hit .329 with 40 home runs and 102 runs batted in. He also played in another World Series in 1975, against the Cincinnati Reds. Again, the Red Sox came up a game short, losing four games to three.

In 1978, the Red Sox tied the New York Yankees for first place in the American League Eastern Division and played them in a one-game playoff. Although Carl hit a first-inning home run, the Red Sox lost 5 to 4.

In big games, Carl always hit well. His regular season career batting average was a respectable .285, but in playoffs, the World Series, and All-Star contests, he hit over .340. His achievements were all the more remarkable because he was not a gifted, all-around athlete. Carl made up for his lack of speed and strength by his almost obsessive determination to improve every facet of his game.

Carl's commitment attracted widespread attention after the first game of the 1967 World Series. Having gone hitless against St. Louis Cardinal ace pitcher Bob Gibson, Carl took extra batting practice. Sports reporters thought it remarkable, but Carl had taken extra hitting after games on several occasions.

Always intense, Carl constantly worked on his batting stance and swing. He wanted to be perfect and was willing to work many hours a day to adjust his approach to hitting.

Carl played his last major league season in 1983.

Summary

Carl Yastrzemski considered himself to be a craftsman. He endured because he always sought to improve his skills. He led by example, playing with injuries and sacrificing his personal statistics for the good of the team. Fans respected him as much for his drive to excel as for his achievements.

Larry Gragg

2847

STATISTICS

Season	Games	At Bats	Hits	Doubles	Triples	Home Runs	Runs	Runs Batted In	Batting Average	Slugging Average
1961	148	583	155	31	6	11	71	80	.266	.396
1962	160	646	191	43	6	19	99	94	.296	.469
1963	151	570	**183**	**40**	3	14	91	68	**.321**	.475
1964	151	567	164	29	9	15	77	67	.289	.451
1965	133	494	154	**45**	3	20	78	72	.312	**.536**
1966	160	594	165	**39**	2	16	81	80	.278	.431
1967	161	579	**189**	31	4	**44**	**112**	121	**.326**	**.622**
1968	157	539	162	32	2	23	90	74	**.301**	.495
1969	162	603	154	28	2	40	96	111	.255	.507
1970	161	566	186	29	0	40	**125**	102	.329	**.592**
1971	148	508	129	21	2	15	75	70	.254	.392
1972	125	455	120	18	2	12	70	68	.264	.391
1973	152	540	160	25	4	19	82	95	.296	.463
1974	148	515	155	25	2	15	**93**	79	.301	.445
1975	149	543	146	30	1	14	91	60	.269	.405
1976	155	546	146	23	2	21	71	102	.267	.432
1977	150	558	165	27	3	28	99	102	.296	.505
1978	144	523	145	21	2	17	70	81	.277	.423
1979	147	518	140	28	1	21	69	87	.270	.450
1980	105	364	100	21	1	15	49	50	.275	.462
1981	91	338	83	14	1	7	36	53	.246	.355
1982	131	459	126	22	1	16	53	72	.275	.431
1983	119	380	101	24	0	10	38	56	.266	.408
Totals	3,308	11,988	3,419	646	59	452	1,816	1,844	.285	.462

NOTE: Boldface indicates statistical leader.

MAJOR LEAGUE RECORDS

★ Most intentional walks, 190
★ Highest fielding percentage, season, 1.000 (1977) (record shared)

AMERICAN LEAGUE RECORDS

★ Most consecutive seasons playing 100 games, 20

HONORS AND AWARDS

1963, 1965-79, 1982-83	American League All-Star Team
1963, 1965, 1967	*The Sporting News* American League All-Star Team
1963, 1965, 1967-69, 1971, 1977	American League Gold Glove Award
1963, 1965, 1967-69, 1971, 1977	*The Sporting News* American League All-Star Fielding Team
1967	American League Most Valuable Player
1967	*The Sporting News* Major League Player of the Year
1967	*The Sporting News* American League Player of the Year
1967	Associated Press Male Athlete of the Year
1967	*Sports Illustrated* Sportsman of the Year
1967	Hickok Belt
1970	All-Star Game Most Valuable Player
1989	National Baseball Hall of Fame
—	Uniform number 8 retired by the Boston Red Sox

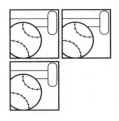

CY YOUNG

Sport: Baseball

Born: March 29, 1867
Gilmore, Ohio
Died: November 4, 1955
Peoli, Ohio

Early Life

Cy Young was born Denton True Young on March 29, 1867, in Gilmore, Ohio. His middle name was said to be the last name of a soldier who had saved his father's life in the Civil War.

When "Dent," as he was called in his youth, was growing up, much of America was agricultural. In fact, it was on these wide open fields that the game of baseball began to be played. When Dent was old enough, he began working as a farmer and a rail-splitter in Gilmore, which was rich Ohio farmland. It was also in these fields that he first played baseball with the other farmhands.

The Road to Excellence

By 1890, Dent was a strapping 6-foot 2-inch, 210-pound twenty-three-year-old. His fast pitch was the talk of the county, and Dent wanted to use it in organized competition. At first, his parents felt he should remain a farmer, but reluctantly, they gave in, and Dent got a tryout with the Canton, Ohio, team in the Tri-State League.

It was at that tryout that Denton Young was first called "Cy," although there are at least two different stories behind the nickname. According to one story, Dent reported to the Canton team in clothes so ill-fitting that he was at once branded as a hick fresh off the farm and given the name "Cyrus." According to another story, Young's

warm-up pitches were so powerful that they left the fence of the ballpark looking like a cyclone had hit it, and a sportswriter began calling the new pitcher "Cyclone" Young.

In midseason, Cy pitched a no-hitter against McKeesport, striking out 18 batters. News of the game spread to the Cleveland Spiders of the National League, which paid Canton $250 for the big right-hander.

The Emerging Champion

In his first major league game, Cy pitched a 3-hitter for Cleveland against Chicago. It was a promise of things to come.

Cy Young blossomed in 1892, winning 36 games while losing just 12. He also led the league in earned run average (ERA), allowing only 1.93 earned runs per game. Over the next eight seasons, Cy won an incredible 237 games, winning better than 30 games a season three times—astronomical numbers for a pitcher in any era.

Baseball was a different game in the late 1800's from what it is today, and Cy had to adapt to a number of rule changes in the middle of those amazing eight years. For instance, in 1892, pitchers threw off a flat dirt surface 50 feet from the catcher; the following season, the distance was increased to the modern-day 60 feet, 6 inches, and a pitchers "mound" was allowed.

Another change that came to baseball during this time was the start of a new major league, the American League, in 1900. In 1899, the Spiders had moved from Cleveland to St. Louis. The Boston team, soon to become known as the Red Sox, lured Cy, now thirty-four years old, to the new

league by offering more money and a cooler climate. In 1901, Cy led the league in victories, strikeouts, and ERA.

In 1903, Boston finished first in the American League and Pittsburgh was the top team in the National League. At the end of the season, the two teams agreed to play each other to see which was better, and the World Series was born. Cy, who had won the most games of any American League pitcher in each of the last three years, started three games in that best-of-nine Series, losing the first game but winning the fifth and seventh to help Boston win the Series, 5-3.

The following year, some believed Cy, at age thirty-seven, was washed up. Rube Waddell, the twenty-eight-year-old pitching star for the Philadelphia Athletics, promised he would win when the two pitched against each other. The matchup occurred on May 5, 1904, and Cy pitched a perfect game, retiring all 27 batters who faced him, as Boston won, 3-0. Cy pitched three no-hitters during his major league career, the last on June 8, 1908, at age forty-one.

Cy credited his longevity to farming. He continued to swing an ax as a rail-splitter in the off-season and said his farm chores strengthened his back and legs.

In 1909, Cy was sold to Cleveland of the American League, where he played two seasons, winning 19 games his first year there. In 1911, he went to Boston of the National League and retired at the end of the season after twenty-two years in the major leagues.

Continuing the Story

During Cy Young's career, relief pitchers were not commonly used; the pitcher who started the game usually finished it. The spitball was legal, and the curveball and the slider, two modern-day pitches that put a great strain on the arm, had not been developed. For these reasons, many of Cy's records will most likely never be broken. He finished his career with more wins (511) and more losses (315) than any pitcher in baseball. He also completed more games (750) and pitched more innings (7,356) than any pitcher ever has and probably ever will. He won at least 20 games in sixteen seasons, and won 30 or more in five of those years.

After he retired, Cy went back to Ohio and to farming. When his wife died in 1933, he sold his land and went to live with friends who were also farmers. In 1937, Cy was elected to the National Baseball Hall of Fame.

Cy still loved baseball and was a frequent visitor to the ballpark at Cleveland Indians games until his death on November 4, 1955, in Peoli, Ohio, at the age of eighty-eight. The next year, baseball began giving out the Cy Young Award for pitching excellence at the end of every season.

Summary

Cy Young grew up with baseball and became one of its legends. He came to the sport when both baseball and he were fresh off the farm and became one of its star players who helped make the game popular with fans. Cy was baseball's most indestructible pitcher; he threw more innings and won more games than anyone else. His records are so secure that the name baseball chose for the prize given annually to the best pitchers in both leagues is the Cy Young Award.

W. P. Edelstein

STATISTICS

Season	Games	Games Started	Games Completed	Innings Pitched	Hits Allowed	Walks	Strikeouts	Wins	Losses	Saves	Shutouts	ERA
1890	17	16	16	147.2	145	30	39	9	6	0	0	3.47
1891	55	46	43	423.2	431	140	147	27	22	2	0	2.85
1892	53	49	48	453	363	118	168	36	12	0	**9**	**1.93**
1893	53	46	42	422.2	442	103	102	34	16	1	1	3.36
1894	52	47	44	408.2	488	106	101	26	21	1	2	3.94
1895	47	40	36	369.2	363	75	121	**35**	10	0	4	3.24
1896	51	46	42	414.1	477	62	**140**	28	15	3	5	3.24
1897	46	38	35	335	391	49	88	21	19	0	2	3.79
1898	46	41	40	377.2	387	41	101	25	13	0	1	2.53
1899	44	42	40	369.1	368	44	111	26	16	1	4	2.58
1900	41	35	32	321.1	337	36	115	19	19	0	4	3.00
1901	43	41	38	371.1	324	37	**158**	**33**	10	0	5	**1.62**
1902	45	43	41	384.2	350	53	160	**32**	11	0	3	2.15
1903	40	35	34	341.2	294	37	176	**28**	9	2	7	2.08
1904	43	41	40	380	327	29	200	26	16	1	**10**	1.97
1905	38	33	32	320.2	248	30	210	18	19	0	4	1.82
1906	39	34	28	287.2	288	25	140	13	21	2	0	3.19
1907	43	37	33	343.1	286	51	147	21	15	1	6	1.99
1908	36	33	30	299	230	37	150	21	11	2	3	1.26
1909	35	34	30	295	267	59	109	19	15	0	3	2.26
1910	21	20	14	163.1	149	27	58	7	10	0	1	2.53
1911	18	18	12	126.1	137	28	55	7	9	0	2	3.78
Totals	906	815	**750**	**7,356**	7,092	1,217	2,796	**511**	315	16	76	2.63

NOTE: Boldface indicates statistical leader.

MAJOR LEAGUE RECORDS

★ Most victories, 511
★ Most losses, 315
★ Most innings pitched, 7,356
★ Most complete games, 750

HONORS AND AWARDS

1937	National Baseball Hall of Fame
—	After each season, and in honor of Cy Young, the Baseball Writers Association of America presents the Cy Young Award to the best pitcher from each league. This award was originated in 1956.

SHEILA YOUNG

Sports: Speed skating and Cycling

Born: October 14, 1950
Birmingham, Michigan

Early Life

Sheila Young was born on October 14, 1950, in Birmingham, Michigan, not far from the city of Detroit, where the Young family eventually moved. Her parents were both sports-minded; they were champion cyclists and outstanding skaters.

Sheila's father, Clair, founded the Wolverine Sports Club, devoted to developing talent in skating and cycling. Sports, he said, "kept my family together [and were] a terrific influence in bringing up my kids." Sheila got her early training at the Sports Club.

She was given her first pair of skates when she was two. She waited till she was nine, though, before she started skating. "I wasn't that interested in skating when I was little," Sheila remembered. "The family would take off; I didn't want to go."

Once Sheila decided to try skating, the speed fascinated her. "I love the feeling of going fast," she explained.

The Road to Excellence

Sheila was soon winning junior skating championships. A top-notch coach, Peter Schotting, was impressed with Sheila's stamina and style. He sparked her competitive spirit when he told her, "Train with me for a year, and you'll be a world champion."

Schotting's training plan included four hours of skating a day, as well as cycling, jogging, sprinting, and dry-land exercises such as the duckwalk, an exercise performed with the upper body parallel to the ground and the legs bent at the knees.

While training, Sheila had little time for the activities that normally absorb teenagers. Her best friends became the girls she competed with on weekends, who lived in other towns.

While still in high school, Sheila finished second in the U.S. National Outdoor Speed Skating Championships. She placed first in 1970 and again in 1971, and won membership on the 1972 U.S. Olympic team.

The Emerging Champion

At the 1972 Winter Olympic Games in Japan, Sheila missed winning the bronze medal in the 500-meter race by a mere .08 of a second. The very next year, however, was a triumphant one for her. She captured the world championship in speed skating and set a world record for the 500-meter sprint at 41.8 seconds. Skating was not her only claim to fame, though; six months later, Sheila became the first American woman in fifty years to win the world track cycling championship. To everyone's surprise, she overcame the titleholder, as well as injury; with startling determination, she raced the final match with cuts on her arms and legs, along with a deep gash in her scalp. With that victory, Sheila had become the first female athlete to achieve world-class titles in two different sports in the same year.

In 1974, a fall in the sprint races deprived Sheila of a second world championship in speed skating. Demonstrating her never-say-die spirit, she rallied and regained her title the following year.

The 1976 Olympics in Austria brought Sheila the distinction of being the first U.S. athlete to

2853

take home three medals from the Winter Games. Capturing the gold in the 500-meter race, she also won the silver in the 1,500-meter course and the bronze in the 1,000-meter. After her third medal, she was surprised by a congratulatory call from President Gerald Ford.

Sheila's sleek outfit for the Olympic meet also won her a nickname: "The American Frogman." Wearing tight clothes helped her to cut down wind resistance and thus increase speed. "I never wear socks," Sheila explained. "With my bare toes, I have a better rapport with my skates. I can really feel them."

As a bonus, Sheila broke Anne Henning's Olympic record with a time of 42.76 seconds in the 500-meter race. Later that year, she set a world record in the 500-meter course at 40.68 seconds.

A month after Sheila's big Olympic win, she captured her third world sprint speed skating title. That year, 1976, she also won the world title in track cycling, as she beat the favorite in the finals. For the second time, Sheila's daring and determination had made her a double world champion.

Continuing the Story

After her Olympic and world championships in 1976, Sheila announced her retirement from amateur sports competition. That summer, she married Jim Ochowicz, an Olympic cyclist.

In 1978, Sheila and Jim moved to Lake Placid, New York, where Sheila went to work for the U.S. Olympic Organizing Committee. She kept in shape cycling and jogging, and in the fall of 1980 she began training seriously again for a chance to compete in the 1984 Winter Olympics in Yugoslavia.

Sheila had set herself a daunting challenge. "You have to have a certain explosiveness in competition," she acknowledged. "It's hard to get that back."

At the age of thirty and the mother of a two-year-old, Sheila placed first in the U.S. sprint championships for a spot on the national team. Sheila's comeback however, provoked controversy. Her amateur status was in question: Since her Olympic victory, she had been paid $12,500 to appear in ads for Kellogg's Corn Flakes, as well as in the television programs *Superstars* and *Challenge of the Sexes*.

Determined to compete again, Sheila agreed to turn over her earnings in commercial sports to the International Speedskating Association. She was willing to make the sacrifice for the chance to strive again athletically. "My sports have been terrific to me," she explained.

Although Sheila failed to make the 1984 Olympic team, her place in skating history was secure. In May, 1991, she was inducted into the Amateur Skating Union's Speedskating Hall of Fame.

Summary

Every athlete needs to stay in shape. Sheila Young turned this necessity into an opportunity. She translated her cycling practice into a shot at achievement and acclaim. Twice capturing world championships in more than one sport in the same year, breaking records as she blazed trails, Sheila illuminated the peaks the human body and spirit, working in exquisite harmony, can reach.

Amy Adelstein

MAJOR CHAMPIONSHIPS

Year	Competition	Event	Place
1972	Olympic Games	500m	4th
1973, 1975-76	World Speed Skating Championships	—	1st
1973, 1976	World Track Cycling Championships	—	1st
1976	Olympic Games	500m	Gold
		1,000m	Bronze
		1,500m	Silver

HONORS, AWARDS, AND RECORDS

1973	Set a world record in the 500-meter sprint (41.8 seconds)
1976	Set a world record in the 500-meter sprint, 42.76 seconds, then lowered that mark to 40.68 seconds the same year
1991	Amateur Skating Union Speedskating Hall of Fame

ROBIN YOUNT

Born: September 16, 1955
Danville, Illinois

Early Life

Robin R. Yount was born on September 16, 1955, in Danville, Illinois. When he was a year old, his family moved to Los Angeles, California, where his father, Phil, took a job as an aerospace engineer. Robin grew up in an affluent community in the San Fernando Valley.

Even though neither of Robin's parents was athletic, Robin and his two older brothers played sports constantly. The Younts' huge backyard served as a baseball diamond, football field, and golf course. Robin exhibited a natural athletic ability almost from the beginning. He started playing golf at the age of nine and began hitting holes-in-one four years later, even though he had had no formal training. At age eleven, he advanced to the more dangerous sport of motorcycle racing and began winning trophies in moto-cross events at age thirteen. Phil Yount explained Robin's success by pointing out that Robin first made up his mind to do something and then he did it.

The Road to Excellence

Robin could have become a professional golfer if baseball had not captured his interest. When he was in junior high school, he completely demolished (through overuse) a batting cage that his father had built for him. In high school, he was named the outstanding baseball player in Los Angeles. His role model during these years was his older brother, Larry, who had a brief career as

a pitcher for the Houston Astros.

Robin began playing baseball professionally in his senior year, when he was picked in the first round of the 1973 draft by the Milwaukee Brewers. He spent only one year in the Class A New York-Pennsylvania League before the Brewers chose him as their starting shortstop. The manager, Del Crandall, was so impressed with Robin's fielding and hitting ability that he completely disregarded the fact that Robin was only eighteen years old.

Robin was still developing as a player during his first four seasons with the Brewers. He batted better than .250 each year and had a strong .288 in 1977. Although he made 44 errors in 1975, he had clearly improved as a fielder three years later.

In 1978, Robin was faced with the most crucial decision of the year. Dissatisfied with his hitting and stricken with tendinitis in his ankles, he was not sure that he wanted to sign his contract in the spring. He was also tempted to move to California so that he could be with his girlfriend, Michelle. It was only when she agreed to marry him later that year that he decided to continue his baseball career.

The Emerging Champion

Robin has always enjoyed playing baseball, but he admits that he had the most fun in the major leagues in 1982. In that year, he hit 29 home runs and won the American League Most Valuable Player award. Robin also helped the Brewers win the division title by hitting two home runs in the fourth game of the playoffs. Even though the Brewers eventually lost the World Series to the St.

2857

Louis Cardinals, Robin has fond memories of the spirit of camaraderie that held the team together. To Robin, who has always been a team player, the 1982 Brewers was the ideal team.

After the 1982 World Series, Robin was well on his way to becoming one of the best all-around shortstops in baseball. In 1984 and 1985, however, he suffered two shoulder injuries that almost ended his career. Robin returned to baseball after surgery but was told that his arm would never be strong enough for him to play shortstop again. Robin resisted the temptation to quit playing entirely; instead, he moved to center field where he has become a superb defensive player. He has learned to live with the harsh reality of never being able to play his favorite position again.

Despite his injuries, Robin still believed that he could be a productive batter, and he proved that he was in 1987. By the end of August, he was batting .312 and had driven in 103 runs. He was the first Brewers player to have 100 runs batted in since 1983. He also hit 21 homers, his highest total since 1982. He left no doubt at the end of what became one of his best seasons that he was still physically able to do the job.

Continuing the Story

Miraculously, Robin has managed to remain humble even as he continues to break records well into his thirties. After hitting his 945th RBI and breaking the Brewers' old record of 944, Robin could not understand why his teammates wanted him to keep the ball. He was more pleased with giving the Brewers a needed run than with setting a record. Then, in 1989, he became the fifth-youngest player to reach 2,500 hits. Robin told reporters afterward that the hit was impor-

tant because it drove in two runs. Personal statistics are not important to Robin. He has been able to get that many hits, he says, only because he has played a long time.

Although Robin has tended to downplay his own accomplishments, the baseball world has not. In 1989, he was once again selected as the Most Valuable Player (MVP) in the American League, joining Stan Musial and Hank Greenberg as the only players ever to win the MVP award at two positions. In typical fashion, though, Robin insisted that the award also belonged to his teammates, the Brewers organization, and his fans.

As Robin approaches the end of his career, his primary goal is not to break any more records or win any more awards. His fondest wish is to play in the World Series once more before he retires. In fact, in 1989, he filed for free agency and would have left the Brewers if he thought his chances of playing in another World Series would improve by going elsewhere. Meanwhile, Robin is content to occupy himself by giving one hundred percent to his game and riding dirt bikes in his spare time.

Summary

Robin Yount has proven to be one of the Milwaukee Brewers' most consistent performers since making the club as an eighteen-year-old shortstop in 1973. Former Brewers manager Tom Trebelhorn wanted every one of his players to be like Robin. Unlike many players, who long to be standouts, Robin is happy to be a team player and is concerned foremost with living up to his own high standards of performance. He is not as entertaining as some of the more flamboyant players, but he is indispensable to his team.

Alan Brown

STATISTICS

Season	Games	At Bats	Hits	Doubles	Triples	Home Runs	Runs	Runs Batted In	Batting Average	Slugging Average
1974	107	344	86	14	5	3	48	26	.250	.346
1975	147	558	149	28	2	8	67	52	.267	.367
1976	161	638	161	19	3	2	59	54	.252	.301
1977	154	605	174	34	4	4	66	49	.288	.377
1978	127	502	147	23	9	9	66	71	.293	.428
1979	149	577	154	26	5	8	72	51	.267	.371
1980	143	611	179	**49**	10	23	121	87	.293	.519
1981	96	377	103	15	5	10	50	49	.273	.419
1982	156	635	**210**	**46**	12	29	129	114	.331	**.578**
1983	149	578	178	42	**10**	17	102	80	.308	.503
1984	160	624	186	27	7	16	105	80	.298	.441
1985	122	466	129	26	3	15	76	68	.277	.442
1986	140	522	163	31	7	9	82	46	.312	.450
1987	158	635	198	25	9	21	99	103	.312	.479
1988	162	621	190	38	**11**	13	92	91	.306	.465
1989	160	614	195	38	9	21	101	103	.318	.511
1990	158	587	145	17	5	17	98	77	.247	.380
1991	130	503	131	20	4	10	66	77	.260	.376
Totals	2,579	9,997	2,878	518	120	235	1,499	1,278	.288	—

NOTE: Boldface indicates statistical leader.

HONORS AND AWARDS

1980, 1982-83	American League All-Star Team
1982, 1989	American League Most Valuable Player
1982	*The Sporting News* Major League Player of the Year
1982	American League Gold Glove Award
1982	Seagram's Seven Crowns of Sports Award

BABE DIDRIKSON ZAHARIAS

Sports: Track and field, Golf, Basketball, and Softball

Born: June 26, 1914
Port Arthur, Texas
Died: September 27, 1956
Galveston, Texas

Early Life

Mildred Ella Didriksen was born on June 26, 1914, in Port Arthur, Texas. She was the sixth of seven children born to Ole and Hannah Didriksen (she changed the "e" in her parents' Norwegian name to an "o" later in her life).

Mildred's parents were poor but strict. Her father had worked as a cabinetmaker on ships at sea while in Norway but now made a meager wage as a furniture refinisher. Her mother was a housekeeper and took in washing and ironing from neighbors to help the family survive. The family moved to Beaumont, Texas, when Mildred was three years old.

Mildred's father was a fitness fanatic. He required each of his seven children to exercise and to play sports. Her mother had been one of the best skaters and skiers while in Norway. Mildred's father built playing fields and exercise equipment of all kinds for his children. With four brothers and two sisters plus many neighbor boys and girls in the yard at all times, Mildred learned to compete against boys in numerous sports.

Some reports claim Mildred was called Babe because she was the baby of the family. Others say it was because she hit a baseball like Babe Ruth.

The Road to Excellence

Through her years at Magnolia Grade School, Babe competed on even terms with the boys. She also played the harmonica for three years on a weekly radio show and was an excellent student. She won first prize at the Texas State Fair for a dress she made.

While at South Junior High School, Babe decided she wanted to become the greatest athlete who ever lived, and while playing basketball for Beaumont Senior High School, she made All-City and All-State.

Colonel Melvin J. McCombs, the coach of one of the best women's amateur basketball teams in the nation, convinced Babe to play for his team, the Golden Cyclone Athletic Club, which was sponsored by the Employers Casualty Company of Dallas. The Employers Casualty Company hired Babe as a typist and to play on their basketball, track, and other sport teams. She became an All-American in basketball while leading the team to the national championship. She also won medals in ice-skating and swimming.

The Emerging Champion

In the spring of 1929, Babe talked Mr. McCombs into starting an Employers Casualty Company track team because she wanted to try track. She threw herself into practice in the afternoon and again at night. She wanted to try every event. In 1929, track competitors were allowed to enter as many events as they desired. By this time Babe had grown into a 5-foot 4-inch, 105-pound, well-muscled athlete.

Babe won eight of the ten events she entered in the Texas State Track and Field Championships. In 1929, she broke the world javelin record with a throw of 133 feet 3¼ inches. In 1930, her baseball

2861

throw of 296 feet set a women's record.

In 1932, Babe became the best female track and field athlete in the United States and then in the world. The National Championships and the 1932 Olympic trials were combined into one meet held at Northwestern University.

Babe entered the meet as a one-woman team representing the Employers Casualty Company. She entered eight of the ten events, winning five and placing in two others. She set world records in the hurdles (12.1 seconds) and the javelin (139 feet 3 inches) and tied Jean Shiley with a world-record high jump (5 feet 3¾ inches). Babe scored 30 points and won the meet by herself, beating the second-place team (twenty-two women representing the Illinois Athletic Club) by eight points.

Continuing the Story

A few weeks later, Babe was off to Los Angeles for the 1932 Olympics. In 1932, women's Olympic track and field consisted of only five individual events. Each person was allowed to enter no more than three of the events. Babe chose the javelin, the hurdles, and the high jump.

Babe's first throw in the javelin was a world record (143 feet 4 inches). In the 80-meter hurdles, she broke a second world record (11.7 seconds). In the high jump, she tied for first place at a world record height (5 feet 5 inches). A judge disqualified her from first place, contending that her head passed over the bar before the rest of her body, which was not allowed in those days. She settled for the silver medal.

Babe's great dedication to practice, determination to succeed, and athletic ability resulted in her winning her first of six Associated Press Female Athlete of the Year Awards. She had become a star.

At first, Babe tried many different activities, attempting to cash in on her Olympic fame. She is said to be the greatest woman athlete of all time. She toured the country with Babe Didrikson's All-Americans, a basketball team. She was the only woman on the team. She traveled with the bearded House of David baseball team. She was a pitcher and the only woman on the team. She pitched in a major league baseball exhibition game during spring training.

After the Olympics, Babe decided to become a golfer. She practiced and practiced, sometimes for as many as ten hours a day. Often her hands would bleed, and she would bandage them and keep practicing. She was a long hitter from the beginning, often out-driving men players. Her short game needed a great amount of practice, and she was determined to become a good player around the greens and to control her tee shots.

Babe entered her first golf tournament in 1934, shooting a 77 to win first place. During the next twenty years, Babe would win fifty-three major golf tournaments all over the world. Between 1946 and 1947, she won seventeen straight titles, a record no one else has come close to before or since.

In 1938, Babe met and married a wrestler, George Zaharias. He gave up his career to help Babe continue her golf career.

Babe was voted the Outstanding Female Athlete of the first half of the twentieth century. In 1953, she learned that she had cancer. Through several cancer operations, she fought the disease valiantly. She won the United States Women's Open and four other golf tournaments in 1954. After a courageous fight, Babe Didrikson Zaharias died of cancer on September 27, 1956.

Summary

Babe Didrikson Zaharias became an outstanding athlete because of her intense desire to be the best woman athlete in the world. Her parents gave her a good foundation and, using her great competitive desire, she achieved her goal.

Walter R. Schneider

MAJOR CHAMPIONSHIPS

Year	Competition	Event	Place	Time/Distance/Height
1930	National AAU Outdoor Championships	Javelin throw	Gold	133′3″
1931	National AAU Outdoor Championships	80m hurdles	Gold	12.1
		Long jump	Gold	17′ 11½″
1932	Olympic Games	80m hurdles	Gold	11.7 OR
		High jump	Silver	5′5″
		Javelin throw	Gold	143′4″ WR, OR
1932	National AAU Outdoor Championships	80m hurdles	Gold	12.1
		High jump	Gold	5′ 3¾″ WR
		Shot put	Gold	39′ 6¼″
		Javelin throw	Gold	139′ 3″ WR

NOTE: OR = Olympic Record. WR = World Record.

MAJOR CHAMPIONSHIP VICTORIES (GOLF)

1940, 1944-45, 1950	Western Open
1946	U.S. Women's Amateur
1947	British Open Amateur Championship
1947, 1950, 1952	Titleholders Championship
1948, 1950, 1954	U.S. Women's Open

OTHER NOTABLE VICTORIES

1940, 1944, 1951-52	Texas Open
1948, 1950-51, 1954	All-American Open
1948, 1951	World Championship
1949	Eastern Open
1953	Babe Zaharias Open

RECORDS

★ Set the women's world record in the javelin throw in 1929 (133′ 3¼″)
★ First American golfer to capture the British Open Amateur Championship since it was first played in 1893

HONORS AND AWARDS

1932, 1945-47, 1950, 1954	Associated Press Female Athlete of the Year
1950	Associated Press Outstanding Female Athlete of the Half-Century
1951	LPGA Hall of Fame
1954	GWAA Ben Hogan Award
1954	GWAA Richardson Award
1954	LPGA Vare Trophy
1957	USGA Bobby Jones Award
1974	National Track and Field Hall of Fame
1974	PGA/World Golf Hall of Fame
1977	PGA Golf Hall of Fame
1980	Sudafed International Women's Sports Hall of Fame Pioneer
1983	U.S. Olympic Hall of Fame

MILESTONES

★ LPGA leading money-winner four consecutive years (1948-51)
★ Garnered thirty-one victories out of one hundred twenty-eight LPGA events during her eight-year career
★ Founder and Charter Member of the LPGA
★ Named "Golfer of the Decade" (1948-57) by *Golf* Magazine

EMIL ZATOPEK

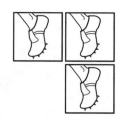

Sport: Track and field (long-distance runs and marathon)

Born: September 19, 1922
Koprivnice, Moravia,
Czechoslovakia

Early Life

Emil Zatopek was born on September 19, 1922, in Koprivnice, Moravia, in the northern part of Czechoslovakia. His father worked as a carpenter in a local shoe factory. The family was so poor that when Emil was a child, his father would scold him for running because running wore his shoes out faster than if he walked.

After graduating from secondary school, Emil considered applying to the teacher's training school, but the competition to get in was so great that he felt he would not be accepted. Therefore, he went to work in a shoe factory in Zlin and attended night classes at the Zlin Technical School. Originally, his job was to attach rubber soles to tennis shoes, but he was transferred to another department in which he ground silica to dust. This left him covered with the dust, which he would breathe into his lungs. Aware that this could be harmful to his health, Emil applied for a transfer, but it was denied.

The Road to Excellence

At first, Emil did not wish to be a runner. When his employer entered him in a race sponsored by the shoe factory, Emil tried to hide in the library to avoid having to run. When he was spotted and forced to race, he remembered his father's motto: "A thing worth doing, is worth doing well." Therefore, he did his best and came in second in the race. This display of talent so im-

pressed his employer that he was entered in other races and his career as a runner was under way.

After the Germans were driven out of Czechoslovakia at the end of World War II, Emil enlisted in the Czech army and entered officer training school. While the other cadets were relaxing during their free time, Emil used every available moment to train. He was so determined not to miss his workouts that he would run in the rain or through snow if necessary; sometimes it became dark before he finished and he had to use a flashlight to see the path he used for running.

Emil was one of the pioneers of a new type of training for distance running: interval training. Instead of doing long, slow runs in practice to demonstrate that he could complete the distance of the race, he did repeats of very short distances at the pace he hoped to run in the race or faster.

The Emerging Champion

Although his time in the 10,000 meters was less than two seconds off the world record, Emil was not the favorite in that event at the 1948 Olympic Games. Because he lived in a country behind the Iron Curtain, his times were not widely known outside Czechoslovakia. His first-place finish in the 10,000-meter race in an Olympic record time at the 1948 Olympics changed that. When he followed this with a close second-place finish in the 5,000-meter race, he was recognized as one of the world's best runners.

At the Olympics, Emil met the woman who would become his wife. Dana Ingrova, representing Czechoslovakia, placed seventh in the Olympic women's javelin throw. Less than two months

Emil Zatopek leads the way in the homestretch of the 5,000 meters.

after the Olympic Games concluded, they were married.

Although Emil was the best distance runner in the world by 1952, he did not expect to do well at the 1952 Olympic Games because he had been ill with influenza and had not been able to train properly. During the early stages of the 10,000-meter race, he stayed at the back, far behind the leaders, but when he surged to the front during the second half of the race, he left the other runners far behind and won in the Olympic record time of 29 minutes 17 seconds. In the 5,000 meters, Emil appeared to have been beaten until he put on a determined kick in the last 100 meters, which brought him into first place.

Emil's performance in the marathon was the most amazing of all. He had never run the event, he was tired from having run in two events already, and he had to compete against the world record holder, Jim Peters. During the race, Emil was so uncertain as to what pace he should run that he asked Peters if the pace was too fast. Hoping that Emil would speed up and wear himself out, Peters tried to trick Emil by telling him the pace was too slow. Emil did increase his speed but surprised Peters by maintaining the faster pace until the finish. In his first attempt at the distance, Emil not only won an Olympic gold medal, he also set an Olympic record of 2 hours, 23 minutes, and 3 seconds.

Continuing the Story

In the years immediately following the 1952 Olympics, Emil continued to dominate distance running, setting world records at every distance from 3 miles to the marathon. Younger runners, however, imitated his training methods and by 1954 were beginning to defeat Emil, especially at shorter distances. Although he had set a world record in the 5,000 meters earlier in the year in 13 minutes 57.2 seconds, Emil only managed third place in the 1954 European Championships. After having been first in the world at 10,000 meters for seven years, he was ranked only fourth in 1955.

Emil responded to his decline by training even harder. He ran as many as ninety repeats of his 400-meter runs in a day. He even tried to strengthen his leg muscles by running with his wife, Dana, on his shoulders. This plan proved disastrous, as he developed a hernia and could not run for several months. Yet the incident was typical of Emil's willingness to experiment with new training methods in order to improve himself.

Summary

Emil Zatopek was famous for his awkward, ungainly running style. Yet by training harder than his opponents and by using the new interval method of training, he became one of the greatest distance runners of all time.

Harold L. Smith

RECORDS

★ World record at 5,000 meters in 1954 (13:57.2)
★ Five world records at 10,000 meters: 1949 (29:28.2), 1949 (29:21.2), 1950 (29:02.6), 1953 (29:01.6), and 1954 (28:54.2)
★ World record at 6 miles in 1954 (27:59.2)
★ Set 18 world records ranging from 5,000 meters to 30,000 meters
★ National champion 8 times at 5,000 meters and twice at 10,000 meters

---

HONORS AND AWARDS

1949   World Trophy

MAJOR CHAMPIONSHIPS

Year	Competition	Event	Place	Time
1948	Olympic Games	5,000m	Silver	14:17.8
		10,000m	Gold	29:59.6 OR
1950	European Championships	5,000m	Gold	14:03.0
		10,000m	Gold	29:12.0
1952	Olympic Games	5,000m	Gold	14:06.6 OR
		10,000m	Gold	29:17.0 OR
		Marathon	Gold	2:23:03.2 WR, OR
1954	European Championships	5,000m	Bronze	
		10,000m	Gold	28:58.0

NOTE: OR = Olympic Record. WR = World Record.

STEVE ZUNGUL

Sport: Soccer

Born: July 28, 1954
Split, Dalmatia, Yugoslavia

Early Life

Slavisa "Steve" Zungul was born on July 28, 1954, in the coastal city of Split in Dalmatia, Yugoslavia. His father was a semiretired army instructor who was also a commercial fisherman. Steve's talent for soccer was evident when he was very young, and when he was eleven a document was forged to give his age as fifteen so he could play in a youth tournament.

Sometimes Steve would fish with his father on the Adriatic Sea from midnight until five in the morning. At school in the mornings he learned auto mechanics, but nothing could replace his love of soccer, to which he devoted his afternoons and evenings. When he was fifteen, he ran away from home to play in a soccer match. He was gone for a week, to the anger of his family. His mother locked him in his room and told him that there would be no more soccer, but he climbed down two stories on a rope and went to practice.

The Road to Excellence

When Steve was seventeen, he was signed by Hajduk Split, a team in Yugoslavia's first division. Yugoslavia was the only Eastern European country that permitted professional soccer, and Steve was soon making his mark in the game. He scored 250 goals in 350 games with Hajduk Split, helping them to three league championships in six years. In 1978, he was named by *France Football* magazine as one of the six best forwards in Europe. At the time he was also the leading scorer for the Yugoslav national team.

In 1978, Steve was due to report for eighteen months of military service. He decided to leave Hajduk Split and travel to the United States. There he met Don Popovic, who was coach of the New York Arrows in the Major Indoor Soccer League (MISL), which was about to commence its first season. Popovic was also a Yugoslav and a former Hajduk Split player, and he offered Steve a chance to play in a few exhibition games. Steve jumped at the opportunity and quickly made an impact in a new type of soccer, very different from the outdoor game to which he was accustomed. The exhibition games led to a longer stay, and at the end of the 1978-79 season, Steve had scored 43 goals in 18 games. He was only two goals short of being the league's scoring champion.

The Emerging Champion

Steve's phenomenal goal-scoring feats helped the New York Arrows to dominate the MISL in its early years. Steve led them to four successive championships, in 1979, 1980, 1981, and 1982. He became the MISL's all-time leading scorer, with 419 goals and 222 assists. On one occasion he scored three times in thirty-seven seconds. In 1980, he won the league's Triple Crown for most goals, assists, and points. He did it again in 1981-82 and 1984-85.

In addition to his immense natural ability, Steve owed his success to his constant practice and his will to win. He once told a reporter, "I hate to lose; I hate to be beaten at anything. *How* I score goals I cannot tell you; it happens in a dream. It comes from God. But *why* is easy—I will not lose.

2870

It hurts me physically to be defeated." Steve was a hard competitor; he knew that he might come in for some rough treatment from the opposition, but when felled he would simply get up and get on with the game. In his goal scoring, he was just as lethal with either foot, and his positioning was almost perfect, which enabled him to take advantage of rebounds. Steve was a thinker, too. He once said to a young player that when a game was over it was not only the body but also the brain that should be tired.

Steve owed a lot of his success to Arrows coach Don Popovic. Steve regarded him as the best coach in the game. It was a stormy relationship between two outspoken men, but each had confidence in the other.

Steve loved his new home of New York, and the Arrows' fans took him to their hearts. He was known admiringly as the "Lord of All Indoors" and was once described as the Pelé of indoor soccer. "ZSHUN-gul, ZSHUN-gul" the crowd would chant when the Arrows needed a goal. The strategy of the whole team was geared to Steve, and it was quite simple: Get the ball to Steve and let him finish off the move with a goal.

During his years with the Arrows, Steve became a celebrity around New York. Some of the publicity concentrated on his fondness for fast cars and the New York nightlife. It was on the soccer field, however, that he earned his glory.

Continuing the Story

In 1983, Steve was traded to the Golden Bay Earthquakes of the North American Soccer League (NASL). The move gave Steve a chance to play outdoor soccer for the first time in nearly five years. After a few months at Golden Bay, he teamed up again with Popovic, who was hired as coach.

The Golden Bay franchise soon folded, though, so Steve took his talents to the San Diego Sockers, one of the most formidable teams in the MISL. He made a typically dramatic impact, scoring five times in his first match in a 10-2 victory. He also helped the Sockers to the MISL championship in 1985.

After that success, Steve was traded to the Tacoma Stars, where he won his sixth MISL scoring title in 1986. In 1988, Steve was back with San Diego, helping them to win the championship for a record fifth time in 1989. The win was Steve's seventh championship. After helping the Sockers to repeat the feat in 1989-90—although he played in only sixteen games—Steve announced his retirement. During his career he had scored a record 652 goals in the MISL.

Summary

Steve Zungul was the most successful and celebrated player in the history of the MISL. His goal-scoring was prolific: He rarely missed a chance, and he had an almost uncanny knack of knowing in advance where the ball would be. "He's the Nureyev of soccer," said one soccer coach, referring to the great Russian ballet dancer. Like Rudolf Nureyev, Steve was a supreme artist in his chosen profession.

Bryan Aubrey

MILESTONES

★ MISL all-time high scorer (652 goals, 1,123 points)

HONORS AND AWARDS

1971, 1974-75	Yugoslavian League champion
1972-77	Yugoslavian League Cup champion
1975	Yugoslavian League Cup Most Valuable Player
1979-82, 1985, 1989-90	MISL champion
1979-82, 1985, 1986	MISL Most Valuable Player
1980-82, 1985	MISL Playoff Most Valuable Player
1984	NASL Most Valuable Player
1980, 1982, 1985	MISL Triple Crown winner

PIRMIN ZURBRIGGEN

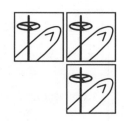

Sport: Skiing

Born: February 4, 1963
Saas-Almagell, Valais, Switzerland

Early Life

Pirmin Zurbriggen was born on February 4, 1963, in the small town of Saas-Almagell, in the canton of Valais, in alpine Switzerland.

Situated near the Italian border, high amid the slopes and pasturelands of the southern Alps, Saas-Almagell is a resort village catering to the tourist crowds that flock to the Alps every year in search of perfect winter sport conditions.

The Zurbriggen name, a common one in the Saas-Valley, has been associated with the hotel trade for generations, and Pirmin's parents were no exception to this tradition. For more than thirty years, Alois and Ida Zurbriggen have owned and operated a small sport hotel called the Lärchenhof.

As a young boy and teenager helping in his parents' hotel, Pirmin learned both the respect that alpiners have for the mountains and the sense of tradition that binds families for many years to their villages.

The Road to Excellence

Because the ski trails that snake through his mountain village started not more than a few yards from his front door, Pirmin developed his enthusiasm for speed skiing at an early age.

Every young person taking up a sport has heroes, forerunners who influence the young athlete by their example. Among Pirmin's were the great Italian skier Gustavo Thoeni, his own countryman Bernhard Russi, and Sweden's legendary Ingemar Stenmark, winner of more than eighty-five World Cup medals. These heroes were to serve Pirmin well on his road to excellence in the demanding alpine disciplines.

Young Pirmin did not have to look very far for the practical encouragement he needed to excel, though. His father, Alois, was a ski racer himself, and although Alois had lost a younger brother in a tragic skiing accident and had never raced after that, he was instrumental in coaching young Pirmin to take up the sport seriously.

With his family's encouragement and his own strong sense of commitment to the challenge of competition, Pirmin excelled from the very beginning.

In 1973, at the age of ten, Pirmin entered his first major competitive event, finishing fourth in the Topolino youth races (Marc Girardelli, later to become his rival in World Cup slalom events, finished second). Two years later, Pirmin won the Ovo Grand Prix and subsequently skied his way to becoming Swiss and European junior downhill champion.

The Emerging Champion

A great honor came to the young skier in 1977 when, at age fourteen, he joined the Swiss B team and came under the coaching of Sepp Stadler. After four years spent developing his skills in the second string, Pirmin moved up to the A team and into the mainstream of World Cup competition. He saw his first World Cup downhill race at Val d'Isere in December, 1980, and later that season he won his first points in the giant slalom at Morzine, France, where he finished seventh.

In World Cup competition, skiers earn points

2874

for their position in the finals of a particular event. At the end of each season, points are tallied up, and the World Cup is awarded to the skier amassing the greatest number of points.

The years following his entry into international competition saw Pirmin advancing steadily in the standings. He finished eleventh in overall points in 1982 and sixth in 1983.

In 1984, Pirmin traveled with the Swiss team to Sarajevo, Yugoslavia, for the Olympic Winter Games. At the Games, Pirmin was competitive in only one event, the downhill, where he finished fourth, just out of medal reach. Upset by this loss, he failed to win medals in any other Olympic event. He recovered substantially, however, and went on to earn a stunning World Cup championship later that year when he finished first in overall points.

At twenty-one, Pirmin had clearly demonstrated that he was a world-class skier capable of dominating a field of diverse and talented competitors.

Continuing the Story

In both the 1985 and 1986 seasons, despite minor injuries, Pirmin skied to second-place finishes in the World Cup overall points standings.

The next year he triumphed over strong international competition to win his second overall World Cup. With this crucial victory, Pirmin solidified his reputation as a master all-event skier, one who excels at all of the alpine disciplines: slalom, giant slalom, super giant slalom, and downhill.

Pirmin has been hailed by his coaches and peers as one of the finest downhill technicians in the history of the sport. Beyond an excellent technique, however, Pirmin possessed an acute sense of concentration. On the slopes, the mild, congenial young man was able to block out all distractions. That concentration earned Pirmin many of his victories.

With two World Cup titles behind him, the twenty-five-year-old was a serious contender for as many as five gold medals at the 1988 Olympics held in Calgary, Canada. (To the four traditional events a fifth had been added, a two-day combined, which took an average score of two separate downhill and slalom races.) Pirmin easily won the downhill gold, flashing across the finish line a full half-second faster than the silver medal winner, his teammate Peter Müller.

Hopes for a record-setting Olympic medal win were dashed, however, when Pirmin fell in the combined slalom race. He took third place in the giant slalom and finished out of medal reach in the other events.

Following his return to the international circuit, he went on to win his third overall World Cup crown. The next season he finished second in overall points.

The following year, 1990, proved to be the pinnacle of Pirmin's career. After a season of outstanding finishes in all disciplines, he skied to his fourth overall World Cup championship, becoming (after his early hero Gustavo Thoeni) only the second man in history to have accomplished this feat. Then, at the age of twenty-seven, and at the absolute height of his career, Pirmin Zurbriggen declared his retirement from the world of competitive skiing.

Summary

Through his dazzling record as a competitive racer, Pirmin Zurbriggen joined an elite group of skiing superstars. He became part of a tradition of excellence that persists not only in the record books, but everywhere young athletes train in hope of victory.

To Pirmin, however, there was another tradition, equally strong, that he knew someday would draw him to it. He always stated that after his skiing days were over he would return to Saas-Almagell to help his parents run their hotel. Now that tradition has claimed him, too.

Tony Abbott

2876

MAJOR CHAMPIONSHIPS

Year	Competition	Event	Place
1981	World Cup	Overall	31st
		Giant slalom	17th
1982	World Cup	Overall	11th
		Giant slalom	6th
		Slalom	33d
1983	World Cup	Overall	6th
		Giant slalom	4th
		Slalom	21st
		Downhill	26th
1984	Olympic Games	Downhill	4th
1984	World Cup	Overall	1st
		Giant slalom	2d
		Slalom	24th
		Downhill	10th
		Combined	2d
1985	World Championships	Giant slalom	2d
		Downhill	1st
		Combined	1st
1985	World Cup	Overall	2d
		Giant slalom	2d
		Slalom	14th
		Downhill	5th
		Combined	9th
1986	World Cup	Overall	2d
		Giant slalom	10th
		Super giant slalom	2d
		Slalom	6th
		Downhill	11th
		Combined	3d
1987	World Championships	Giant slalom	1st
		Super giant slalom	1st
		Downhill	2d
		Combined	2d
1987	World Cup	Overall	1st
		Giant slalom	1st
		Super giant slalom	1st
		Slalom	21st
		Downhill	1st
		Combined	1st
1988	Olympic Games	Giant slalom	Bronze
		Downhill	Gold
1988	World Cup	Overall	1st
1989	World Cup	Overall	2d
1990	World Cup	Overall	1st

RECORD

★ Tied the world record for the most overall World Cup championships (4)

2877

ace: A tennis or volleyball serve delivered so effectively that the opponent cannot even hit it and that scores a point for the server; or a point scored on such a serve.

aft: Toward or near the back of a boat or ship (the stern).

air rifle: A shoulder weapon with a stock and a long barrel and that shoots a small projectile by means of compressed air or carbon dioxide.

All-American: A nationwide honor awarded yearly to the best high school and college athletes in a number of different sports.

all-around: A category of gymnastics competition requiring the performance of routines in all of the individual events. The male and female gymnasts who accumulate the most points at the end are awarded the all-around title, indicative of overall superiority and versatility. Internationally, the men's six events are the floor exercises, the stationary rings, the vault, the pommel horse, the horizontal bar, and the parallel bars. The women's four events are the floor exercises, the balance beam, the vault, and the uneven parallel bars. Competitors are judged on originality, execution, form, artistry, continuity, and degree of difficulty.

all-star game: In team sports, an annual game between the best players from the various leagues or conferences within a sport. Major League Baseball, the National Basketball Association, and the National Hockey League sponsor official All-Star Games; the National Football League's version is the Pro Bowl Game. Major news services such as the Associated Press and United Press International select their own yearly all-star teams, but these selections usually do not involve specially held games.

alley (bowling): A bowling lane.

alley (tennis): The designated area that extends the boundary for doubles matches. In a singles match, hitting the ball into the alley is considered out of bounds.

Alpine skiing: Competitive events consisting of downhill, slalom, giant slalom, and super giant slalom (super G) ski racing.

amateur: Generally, one who competes for prizes rather than money, and who does not attain professional status.

America's Cup: An international series of yacht races, and one of the most prestigious events of its kind. Boats in this class must be 75-foot monohulls with 110-foot masts, and are essentially longer and lighter than the previously used twelve-meter sloops. The races are of two types: match races, which involve only two boats at a time, and fleet races, for all entrants in a round-robin competition. The Cup is defended about every three to four years, and the winner selects the next race location. The America's Cup originated in 1851, in England. The entry from the United States' New York Yacht Club (NYYC) won the race. Sometime thereafter, the owners gave the trophy to the NYYC with the requirement that it be defended whenever challenged, and the trophy was renamed the America's Cup.

anchor leg: The final leg of a relay race; or the athlete who runs this leg.

arrows (archery): The projectiles shot from a bow. Arrows have slender shafts and pointed tips.

arrows (bowling): The seven triangular marks set into the lane just beyond the foul line, which the bowler uses as target points for releasing the ball.

artistic gymnastics: An international Olympic category of events for male and female gymnasts, who compete according to rules prescribed by the International Gymnastics Federation. The men's six events are the floor exercises, the horizontal bar, the parallel bars, the stationary rings, the pommel horse, and the long-horse vault. The women's four events are the floor exercises, the balance beam, the uneven parallel bars, and the side-horse vault.

assist (baseball): Throwing the ball to a teammate on a play that results in a putout.

assist (basketball): Throwing a pass to a teammate who immediately scores a field goal.

assist (hockey): Passing the puck to a teammate who immediately scores a goal, or passing to a teammate who immediately passes the puck to the eventual goal scorer, with not more than two assists per goal being credited.

assist (soccer): Passing the ball to a teammate who scores a goal almost immediately.

Association of Surfing Professionals (ASP) World Tour Championship: The title won by the surfer accumulating the most points on the ASP season tour.

attack: In cycling, a sudden attempt to break away from the *peloton*, the main group of cyclists, in order to seize the lead.

audible: A tactic in football in which the quarterback, after reading the defensive alignment, verbally modifies the offensive play at the line of scrimmage.

Axel jump: A figure skating maneuver achieved by jumping off the forward outside edge of one skate, turning 1½ times in the air, and landing on the backward outside edge of the other skate. Named for its creator, the Norwegian skater Axel Paulsen.

backhand: In tennis or badminton, a stroke that originates from the side of the body opposite the racket hand, or forehand side. As the ball (or shuttlecock) is hit, the back of the racket hand is facing the net.

backspin: The backward rotation on a tennis ball imparted by sweeping the racket face down and under the ball at the point of contact.

backstretch: On a racetrack, the straightaway on the side opposite the homestretch and the finish line.

backstroke: A swimming stroke that requires flutter kicks and alternating pulls with both arms moving up and over the head. Performed on the back.

backward dive: In competitive diving, a maneuver in which the diver stands on the edge of the platform or springboard, facing away from the water, then leaps into the air and rotates backward.

bail: In cricket, one of the two short wooden cylindrical pegs set across the tops of the three stumps that together form the wicket. The batsman is out once the bails are dislodged during play.

balance: As used in bodybuilding, a term that describes a well-proportioned physique. The various muscle groups are in even and pleasing proportion to one another. Among competitive bodybuilders, an especially desirable quality.

balance beam: An event in women's gymnastics involving a combination of dance and tricks (tumbling moves) performed back and forth on the balance beam. The beam itself is sixteen feet long, four inches wide, and raised about four feet off the ground. The exercise lasts from 80 to 105 seconds.

barbell: A steel bar five to seven feet long to which iron weighted plates are attached and securely held by removable metal collars.

bareback riding: A rodeo competition that involves riding an unsaddled wild, bucking horse for eight

2880

seconds, using only one hand to grip a strap attached to the horse's torso. Riders are judged on their control during the ride and how hard the horse bucks. Said to be comparable to riding a jack-hammer with one hand.

barnstorm: A series of exhibition games played by traveling teams from any number of cities or countries.

base stealing: Movement by the base runner in an attempt to catch the defense off guard, and advance from one base to the next without being thrown out. In the event of a hit or error, the advancing runner cannot be credited with a stolen base.

baseline: The back boundary of a tennis court.

baseline player: A tennis player whose game strategy is to stay back at the baseline to hit ground strokes, rarely moving to the net.

bases loaded: Runners occupy first, second, and third base in the same inning in a baseball game.

baton: A hollow cylinder passed in a relay race from one runner to the next upon the completion of each leg except for the final leg.

batsman: The cricket player positioned next to one of the two wickets who tries to hit bowled balls and score runs by advancing from one wicket to the other as many times as possible without being put out.

batting average: A statistical indication of a batter's hitting ability. In baseball, softball, and cricket, a player's average is figured by dividing the total number of hits by the total number of times at bat.

belt: A cloth belt of varying colors worn to indicate a particular level of achievement in judo and other martial arts. In judo, the efficiency grades are of two types: kyu (pupil) and dan (master), the highest grade. Starting with the beginner level, the colors won in judo are white, yellow, orange, green, blue, brown, and black, which signifies the dan or master grade and is itself divided into ten degrees. Sixth-, seventh-, and eighth-degree black belts have the option of wearing a red and white belt; ninth- and tenth-degree black belts may choose a solid red belt.

bench press: In weightlifting, a lift made while lying back on a weight bench and pushing the barbell up from the chest to an overhead position, then lowering it.

bicycle kick: A spectacular soccer maneuver that involves leaping into an upside-down vertical position and using an overhead scissorslike leg motion to kick the ball.

big-bore: In shooting sports, a term that refers to large-caliber firearms; or a caliber larger than .22.

birdie: Finishing a golf hole at one stroke under par for that hole.

blade (fencing): The section of the sword extending from the guard to the tip of the weapon.

blade (rowing): An oar or paddle, or the flat or curved portion of the oar.

bob and weave: A boxer's defensive tactic of rocking his head and torso up and down and back and forth in order to present a moving target that is harder for his opponent to hit.

bobsled: A large, longer racing sled supported underneath by two pairs of runners in tandem, and room for two to four riders. A steering wheel is attached by wires to the two movable front runners. The front rider controls the steering, while the rear rider operates the hand brake.

bobsled run: A narrow, ice-covered chute with high curved walls and numerous banked turns that form the race course in bobsled competition.

body checking: In hockey, to use the body, principally the arms and shoulders, aggressively to block the progress of an opposing puckcarrier or to prevent him from reaching the puck.

bogey: Finishing a golf hole at one stroke over par for that hole.

2881

bomb: A long pass of the football, particularly one that scores a touchdown.

bore: The diameter of the inside of the barrel of a pistol or rifle.

bout: A boxing match. In competition, most bouts are between three and twelve rounds. Each round is three minutes long, with a one-minute rest period in between rounds. How many rounds a bout lasts depends on weight classification and whether the match is amateur or professional.

bow (archery): The shooting device used in archery to propel an arrow. Consists of a long, slender strip of flexible material such as fiberglass or wood, the ends of which are connected by a cord drawn tightly enough to bend the strip.

bow (canoeing/kayaking, yachting): The front of a ship or racing shell.

bowler: The cricket player whose position is similar to a baseball pitcher's. The bowler takes a running start and, using an overhead windmill delivery, hurls the ball at the opposite wicket in an attempt to put out the batsman by dislodging the bail. The bowler is required to keep his throwing arm straight at all times during the delivery.

breakaway: A rider or a group of cyclists that has begun an attack by riding away from another, larger group of cyclists.

breaststroke: A swimming stroke that begins with simultaneous pulls with both arms from in front of the head down to the thighs, a frog kick executed just after the arm pulls end, and a glide through the water with a straight full-body extension. Performed on the stomach.

broken-field runner: In football, a ballcarrier skilled at avoiding opponents in the open field without the usual benefit of teammates blocking for him.

brushback pitch: A high, inside baseball pitch, the only purpose of which is to move the batter away from the plate. An intimidation pitch.

bull riding: A rodeo competition that involves riding a twisting, jumping bull for eight seconds, using only one hand to grip a strap attached to the bull's torso. In major competition, the biggest and fastest bulls weigh more than a ton.

bull's-eye: The center of a target. In archery or shooting sports, hitting the bull's-eye scores the most points.

bully: In field hockey, putting the ball in play by having two opposing players face each other and grapple for possession of it. Similar to the face-off in ice hockey. *See also* face-off.

butterfly: A swimming stroke that requires dolphin kicks and simultaneous pulls with both arms moving up over the head and down under the water. Performed on the stomach.

caliber: The diameter of the inside of the barrel of a pistol or rifle (the bore) measured in hundredths (.22, .44) or thousandths (.357) of an inch.

camel: A skating maneuver performed by spinning the body while in the arabesque position.

canoe: A narrow, lightweight boat that has a pointed bow and stern and is propelled by paddles. Wider than a kayak.

Caprilli method: A revolutionary horse jumping technique devised by Captain Frederico Caprilli, the Riding Master at the Italian Cavalry School in the early 1900's. For a horse to jump well and travel fast in cross-country riding, he noticed, it needs to have the full use of its head, neck, and back. The rider must therefore lean forward in the seat to take the weight off the horse's back, interfering with the horse as little as possible. As a result, horse and rider move as one, giving the impression that the horse is jumping on its own accord. More commonly known as "forward seat" riding.

2882

caps: Appearances in international soccer competition by a player who has been named to his country's national team. Comparable to All-Star team selection.

catch-as-catch-can wrestling: *See* freestyle (wrestling).

century: A score of at least one hundred runs accumulated by a batsman in the space of one inning in a cricket match.

change-up: A baseball or softball pitch that to the batter appears to be a fastball but is actually much slower. A deception pitch used to interrupt the batter's timing.

checkered flag: A flag with black and white squares that is waved to signal the end of an auto race and to indicate the winner.

chip shot: A shot that puts the golf ball onto the green from a point just off the green. Shorter shots of this type are called chip shots. Longer shots are called pitches.

chute (bobsledding): A bobsled run—a narrow, ice-covered passageway with high curved walls and numerous banked turns.

chute (rodeo): A narrow holding pen adjacent to the rodeo arena, used to restrain an animal so that the rider can mount it. As the ride begins, a gate opens into the arena, releasing the animal.

circuit: In sports such as auto racing or cycling, the race course itself. Can also refer to an organized athletic league or conference or a set of leagues or conferences.

classics: The oldest and most important road races of the cycling season. The typical classic race course may be from city to city or point to point and is much shorter in length and duration than the multistage tours.

clean and jerk: In weightlifting, a lift performed by first pulling the barbell up to shoulder level, then pushing it up and over the head and locking the elbows. In the second segment of the lift, the legs are used not only to help hoist the weight but also to lower the body slightly, enabling the lifter to get beneath the barbell.

cleanup hitter: The baseball or softball player who bats fourth in the lineup and who generally is expected to hit well enough to drive in the base runners.

clutch hitter: A baseball or softball batter who is able to get hits and drive in runners, especially at critical times during a game. In general, a "clutch player" in any team sport can perform at the top of his or her game while under intense pressure.

combination: A flurry of different punches thrown rapidly and successively, usually as part of a practiced plan of attack during a boxing match.

completion: A football pass successfully caught by a receiver.

compulsory figures (equestrian): A series of competitive exercises that involve guiding the horse through turns, changes of lead, and tight circles. Also called school figures.

compulsory figures (figure skating): A series of prescribed geometric patterns that a skater must trace with as much precision and grace as possible; these figures (from which figure skating got its name) were dropped from the scoring process in 1990. Also called school figures.

Copa Libertadores: A yearly international soccer tournament between the champions and runners-up from leagues in South American countries to determine the best South American club team.

count: The number of seconds called off by a referee over a fallen boxer. Once the count has begun, the boxer has ten seconds to get back on his feet or the match is over and the opponent wins by a knockout.

counterpunch: To answer or respond immediately to an opponent's lead punch or jab with a punch or a jab during a boxing match.

2883

coxswain: In rowing, a nonrowing crew member who is responsible for setting the rowing pace and maintaining speed and rhythm.

crawl: A swimming stroke that requires flutter kicks and alternating pulls with both arms moving up over the head and down under the water. The fastest of the basic strokes. Performed on the stomach.

crew: The members of a rowing race team, the oarsmen and the coxswain, or any of those who operate a racing shell or a yacht.

criterium: A cycling race of a specified number of laps over a closed course or around an oval track.

cross-country (equestrian): An endurance event in which horse and rider, at various intervals, traverse a course mapped out across the countryside and try to jump over a series of obstacles.

cross-country (skiing): Long-distance races across snow-covered terrain. An event in the Nordic skiing category, which also includes ski jumping.

cross-country (track and field): Long-distance running across dirt roads, wooded areas, grassy fields, and hills.

crossover step: A skating technique used to gain additional thrust while rounding a turn. The skater begins by crossing the outer skate in front of the inner skate, then swinging the inner skate back around and onto the ice while using the outer (first) skate to push off powerfully into the turn.

cup: The small cylindrical chamber into which the golf ball is deposited. Also called the hole.

curve ball: A baseball or softball pitch that veers or breaks downward and to the side. A curve ball thrown by a right-handed pitcher will move away from a right-handed batter.

cut: In sabre fencing, a scoring hit accomplished by striking the opponent with the edge of the weapon.

cut shot: A tactical, deceptive shot used in volleyball by a hitter to misdirect the flight of the ball.

Cy Young award: The highest distinction a major league baseball pitcher can receive. Presented annually to the best pitcher from the National and the American Leagues, as determined by the Baseball Writers Association of America. Named in honor of Hall of Fame pitcher Cy Young, who, with 511 victories, is still professional baseball's all-time wins leader.

dash: A sprint race other than a hurdles or a relay race. In the Olympics, the dashes for both men and women are at distances of one hundred meters, two hundred meters, and four hundred meters.

Davis Cup: An annual international men's tennis tournament between the top sixteen national teams of two to four players each, in both singles and doubles competition. The tournament is played out over the course of a year. Named for American player Dwight Davis.

dead lift: In weightlifting, a lift performed by using the lower back and leg muscles to bring the barbell up to around hip level and then down again.

decathlon: A track and field men's event lasting two days and including the following ten events: the 100- and 400-meter dashes, the 1,500-meter run, the 110-meter hurdles, the long jump, the high jump, the shot put, the discus throw, the javelin throw, and the pole vault. Points are awarded for each event, and the athlete with the most points wins the competition.

decision: A boxing match won on the basis of points scored or the number of rounds won.

defense: In various sports, the attempt to prevent the opposing team from advancing the ball or puck and/or from scoring points, runs, or goals. Playing defense also involves the endeavor to take possession of the ball away from the opponent so that one's own team can advance the ball score. Defense can also refer to the specific game plan used by the team not in possession of the ball. A term used mostly in the context of certain team sports.

definition: As used by bodybuilders, the term means the distinctness or clarity of outline and detail of the exercised muscles. A well-defined bodybuilder will have so little body fat that even the very fine grooves or "striations" of the major muscle groups will be clearly visible.

dig: A successful defensive recovery of a forceful spike or other high-velocity attacking shot in volleyball.

discus throw: A field event that involves throwing a discus for distance. A discus is a disk made of wood or plastic that is thicker at the center than at the perimeter, and about nine inches in diameter and two inches thick at the center.

dojo: In Japanese, *dojo* means "the place of the way." A gymnasium or school where martial arts are taught and practiced.

double: In baseball or softball, a hit that allows the batter to reach second base.

double bogey: Finishing a golf hole at two strokes over par for that hole.

double eagle: Finishing a golf hole at three strokes under par for that hole.

double fault: In a tennis match, the act of committing two foot faults (a foot fault is an illegal placement of at least one of the server's feet) in a row while serving from the same court. A server who commits a double fault loses the point.

double play: In baseball or softball, a defensive move in which two base runners are put out in one play. Perhaps the most frequent double play combination occurs when the shortstop fields a ground ball and tosses it to the second baseman, who tags up and throws the ball to first base for the final putout.

double-team: In various team sports, to guard or defend an opponent with two opposing players simultaneously.

down: The unit in football into which every possession of the ball is divided, four downs per possession. If the offensive team successfully advances the ball at least ten yards, it is immediately awarded another four downs. *See also* first down.

downhill skiing: Gliding down mountain slopes, whether in competition or merely for recreation. Generally, a downhill racer will ski straight down the fall line—the natural slope of the mountain and the shortest distance from point to point—in order to go as fast as possible. The fastest speed event in the Alpine skiing category, which also includes slalom, giant slalom, and super giant slalom ski racing.

draft: The annual method by which professional sports teams select new players. Usually the team with the previous season's worst record is accorded the right to choose first; but this right can be traded away or sold to another team.

drafting: Particularly in auto racing and cycling, the tactic of driving or riding just behind and very close to another car or cyclists in order to take advantage of the slipstream—the tunnel or pocket of reduced air resistance and forward suction created by the moving object in front. Slipstreaming allows the second rider to maintain a certain speed while expending less energy or fuel. *See also* slipstreaming.

dressage: An equestrian event that puts horse and rider through a series of different maneuvers (such as changing gait or walking sideways) to test the horse's ability, training, and obedience and the cooperation between horse and rider. The signals form the rider to the horse should be virtually imperceptible.

dribble (basketball): To bounce the ball across the court using only one hand—the only way a player in possession of the ball can advance.

2885

dribble (soccer): To advance the ball by using the feet to control and direct the ball by lightly tapping it.

drive (basketball): To move rapidly and aggressively with the ball off the dribble, especially as a move toward the baseline or the basket.

drive (golf): Generally, a long-yardage shot hit for distance and accuracy, as from the tee to any place on the fairway and occasionally to the green.

eagle: Finishing a golf hole at two strokes under par for that hole.

earned run: From the baseball or softball pitcher's standpoint, a run scored but not as the result of a defensive error. A statistic credited to the pitcher.

earned run average (ERA): A statistical category that indicates how many earned runs a baseball or softball pitcher allows every nine innings. ERA is figured by dividing the total number of earned runs by the total number of innings pitched, and multiplying the quotient by nine. The result is the pitcher's ERA for one nine-inning game.

eights: A rowing event for racing shells powered by eight oars.

elite: An oarsman who has rowed on a winning boat or racing shell in a championship race. Can also refer to a competition for crews made up of elite-class oarsmen. Generally can refer to the top athletes in a sport.

end zone: The enclosed areas at each end of a football field into which the offensive team must advance the ball to score a touchdown. Also, the area where the goalpost is located.

entry: The last phase of a dive, when the diver enters the water. The less splash created, the better the entry and the higher the final score.

épée fencing: One of the three styles of fencing, in which the épée is used. An épée is a sword equipped with a guard shaped like a small bowl and a fairly rigid blade with a blunted tip and no cutting edge. A thrusting weapon, similar to the foil. *See also* foil fencing, sabre fencing.

equestrian: Refers generally to horseback riding, and also to the competitive events in riding and handling horses such as dressage, cross-country, and show jumping. An equestrian is a person who participates in these sports.

error: A misplay of a batted or thrown ball that is otherwise considered playable and that has allowed a base runner to advance or prevented a putout.

European Cup: A yearly and prestigious international men's tournament between the national soccer champions from all European countries.

even keel: A nautical phrase that describes an evenly balanced boat or ship.

extra-point conversion: A bonus play allowed after each touchdown in football that gives the scoring team a chance to kick a short field goal (good for one extra point) or run or pass the ball into the end zone (good for two extra points).

face-off: In hockey, the referee's act of starting or resuming play by dropping the puck between two opposing players, who then try to control the puck or tip it to a teammate. *See also* bully.

fairway: The expansive, well-maintained portion of a golf course situated between the tee and the putting green, but not including water hazards and sand traps.

fall-away jumper: In basketball, a shot attempted while deliberately moving away from the basket, as opposed to jumping straight up and releasing the shot. *See also* jump shot.

fast break: A basketball play that emphasizes getting the basketball downcourt as fast as possible and anticipating the easy basket while denying the other team the chance to set up defensively. This type of game plan requires strong rebounding, skillful passing, and cooperation from all five players.

fastball: An extremely powerful high-velocity baseball pitch capable of rising or dipping on its way to the plate. The best major league pitchers can throw fastballs ninety to one hundred miles per hour.

Federation Cup: The Davis Cup of women's tennis, started in 1963 by the International Lawn Tennis Federation. Unlike Davis Cup teams, however, Federation Cup teams compete at one location to decide the Cup winner in one week's time. *See also* Davis Cup.

field archery: A series of competitive events set in wooded areas to approximate hunting conditions.

field events: In men's Olympic competition, these include the high jump, the long jump, the triple jump, the pole vault, the shot put, the discus throw, the javelin throw, the hammer throw, and the decathlon. On the women's side, these include the high jump, the long jump, the shot put, the discus throw, the javelin throw, and the heptathlon.

field goal (basketball): A shot, other than a free throw, that falls through the rim. Good for two points if shot in front of the three-point circle, and three points if shot from behind the circle.

field goal (football): A kick made anywhere from behind the line of scrimmage that clears the goalpost crossbars. Good for three points.

fielding: In field hockey, stopping the ball and controlling it.

fielding average: A statistical category that indicates how effectively a baseball fielder performs on defense. Fielding average is figured by dividing the total number of errorless plays by the total number of chances, or attempts.

first-class cricket: The highest level of play in British cricket. Cricket played between the best teams in various countries and universities in the British Commonwealth, each country having its own version of a national championship. The top players from one nation combine to compete against similar teams from other nations in international first-class test matches.

first down: In football, the first of four downs or possessions of the ball by the offensive team. Also, the team in possession of the ball is awarded a "first down" (another four downs) after successfully advancing the ball at least ten yards.

fixed-gear cycling: A track cycling event involving bicycles equipped with only one speed. These bicycles travel only as fast as the cyclist can pedal.

flight shooting: An archery competition that involves shooting arrows for distance rather than at targets.

floor exercise: An event in which a gymnast performs a combination of dance, acrobatic, and tumbling moves utilizing as much as possible the area of a forty-two-foot square mat. Women's floor exercise routines are set to music. Men's routines last 50 to 70 seconds and women's routines last 60 to 90 seconds.

flying camel: A skating maneuver that requires the execution of a flying jump, followed by an airborne camel spin, and a landing that completes the rotation in the camel position. *See also* camel.

foil fencing: One of the three styles of fencing. A foil is a sword equipped with a guard shaped like a small bowl and a flexible blade with a blunted tip and no cutting edge. A thrusting weapon, similar to the épée. *See also* épée fencing, sabre fencing.

forcing the pace: In cycling, to increase the pace to the point that the other cyclists find it hard to keep up.

fore: Toward the front of a boat or ship (the bow).

forehand: In tennis or badminton, a stroke that originates from the same side of the body as the racket hand. As the ball is hit, the palm is facing the net.

Formula One: The highest and fastest level of racing competition on the Grand Prix circuit. Formula One cars are open-wheeled and seat only one driver. They must be built according to "formulas" or specifications that govern details such as engine size, weight, and design which are set by the Fédération Internationale de l'Automobile, the worldwide sanctioning body of auto racing. These cars frequently average speeds well above one hundred miles per hour in competition.

forward dive: In competitive diving, a maneuver in which the diver stands on the edge of the platform or springboard, facing the water, then springs into the air away from the edge and rotates forward.

forward pass: In a football game, a pass thrown in the direction of the opposing end zone.

forward seat riding: *See* Caprilli method.

fours: A rowing event for racing shells powered by four oars.

frame: One of the ten periods or units into which a game of bowling is divided.

free agent: An athlete who is not under contract to any team and who is therefore at liberty to negotiate with any team or organization. A free agent can be a professional athlete whose contract has expired or who has been waived or cut from a team, or an amateur athlete looking to sign with a professional team.

free skating: A long or short skating program consisting of jumps, spirals, dance movements, and other elements designed and choreographed specifically for and/or by the skater. Set to music.

free throw: In basketball, an uncontested shot taken from the free throw line, and which is worth one point per shot made. The result of a personal or technical foul by the opposing team.

freestyle (archery): Target competition in which the archer uses an aiming or sighting device such as a rangefinder or bowsight.

freestyle (skiing): A competition in which the skier is judged in three different events: downhill skiing over rough terrain (mogul), artistic, stylized movements along a gradual slope (ballet), and acrobatic stunts and jumps (aerial).

freestyle (surfing): An event that allows each surfer to select the stunts or maneuvers performed.

freestyle (swimming): A race (such as the 200-meter freestyle) in which the swimmer chooses the stroke to be used. This is almost always the forward crawl, since it is the fastest known stroke. In the individual medley and team relay, the final leg of the race is always designated as freestyle—the swimmer can select any stroke except the butterfly, backstroke, or breaststroke. Freestyle also commonly refers to the forward crawl.

freestyle (wrestling): An event that allows the combatants to use any legal and nondangerous wrestling holds. One of two styles of wrestling featured in the Olympics, the other being Greco-Roman wrestling.

funny car: A highly modified top fuel dragster fitted with a late-model production car body usually made of fiberglass. Nearly as fast as the standard top fuel dragsters, funny cars are powered by a similar type of engine that is mounted in the front and that also runs on nitromethane fuel. Can reach speeds in the range of 290 miles per hour. *See also* top fuel.

furlong: On a horse racing track, a measurement of one-eighth of a mile.

gate: Generally, the money generated by ticket sales at any sporting event.

gate (horse racing): A movable steel contraption the width of the track and fitted with a row of narrow stalls occupied by the horse and jockey at the start of a race. The starting line.

gate (kayaking, skiing, waterskiing, yachting): The markers, poles, or buys through or around which competitors must pass on their way to the finish line.

giant slalom: Similar to the slalom, a skiing race that involves negotiating as fast as possible the downhill weaving pattern of the course. The giant slalom ski run is longer and steeper than that used in slalom, however; the gates used are fewer and spread farther apart. As a result, the run is substantially faster. An event in the Alpine skiing category, which also includes downhill skiing, slalom, and super giant slalom. A race against the clock.

goaltending: An illegal physical interference with a field goal attempt in a basketball game. Both offensive and defensive players can be penalized for this infraction.

Gold Glove Award: An annual distinction given to the best baseball players at each defensive position from both the National and the American Leagues.

Golden Gloves: A nationwide series of amateur boxing elimination tournaments. Regional champions are qualified to compete for the title in their respective weight classifications at the annual Golden Gloves National Championship Tournament.

Grand Prix (auto racing): The most elite series of races in international auto racing competition. A class of races for formula cars. These championship events are now held almost exclusively on specially mapped-out city streets. The driver who accumulates the most points on the Grand Prix circuit is awarded the World Championship of Drivers title at the end of the racing season.

grand prix (equestrian): The expert level of competition at national and international dressage and jumping events. Involves both individual and team competition.

grand slam (baseball): Hitting a home run with runners on first, second, and third base, thus scoring four runs.

Grand Slam (golf): The four major golf tournaments; or the feat of winning them all in the same year. For the men, they are the Masters, the U.S. Open, the British Open, and the Professional Golfers' Association (PGA) Championship. For the women, they are the Ladies Professional Golf Association (LPGA) Championship, the U.S. Women's Open, the Nabisco-Dinah Shore, and the du Maurier Classic.

Grand Slam (tennis): The four major tennis tournaments; or the feat of winning them all in the same year. They are the same for both men and women: the Australian Open, the French Open, the Wimbledon Championships, and the U.S. Open.

Greco-Roman wrestling: One of two styles of wrestling featured in the Olympics, the other being freestyle wrestling. An event in which the combatants cannot apply holds below the waist and cannot use their legs to apply holds or to effect a takedown or a pin.

green: The smooth, usually well-manicured portion of a golf course where the hole is located and where putting is necessary.

ground strokes: A tennis stroke executed by using the racket to strike the ball after it has bounced on the return. Ground strokes are usually hit from the backcourt area or from just beyond the baseline.

half volley: A tennis stroke made by using the racket to strike the ball the instant it bounces up from the ground on the return.

2889

hall of fame: A memorial established to recognize athletes, coaches, and other individuals who have excelled in a particular sport or who have made meritorious contributions to a sport.

hammer throw: A field event that involves throwing the hammer for distance. The hammer is a sixteen-pound metal ball attached to a steel wire with a handle at the end.

handicap: A numerical rating system used as a means of evening out the range of abilities or skill-levels among competitors at certain sports events. In golf, the handicap is the number of strokes a player may legitimately deduct from his or her scorecard after finishing a round or a tournament, as compensation for playing against a better golfer.

hat trick (cricket): A feat accomplished when the bowler dismisses or retires three batsmen on three consecutive balls.

hat trick (ice hockey, soccer): Three goals in one game scored by the same player.

head a shot: To shoot, pass, or clear a soccer ball away from the goal by driving it with the head.

head-of-the-river race: A rowing event in which the participants start the race at different intervals along the course.

heat: A preliminary race used to narrow down the field of competitors to the designated number of finalists.

heavyweight (boxing): A weight classification in professional boxing for athletes weighing more than 190 pounds. In amateur boxing, the maximum limit is 200 pounds.

heavyweight (judo): An international weight classification for athletes weighing more than 209 pounds.

heavyweight (weightlifting): An international weight classification with 242-pound maximum limit.

Heisman Trophy: A yearly award presented to the nation's best college football player as determined by sports media from across the country. Named in honor of former college football coach John W. Heisman. Sponsored by the Downtown Athletic Club of New York. The most coveted individual distinction in college football.

helmsman: In rowing, the crew member who steers the boat or ship by operating the wheel or the tiller.

heptathlon: An individual women's field competition that includes the following seven events: the 100- and 200-meter dashes, the 800-meter run, the high jump, the long jump, the shot put, and the javelin throw. The Olympic heptathlon replaced the pentathlon in 1984.

high bar: *See* horizontal bar.

high jump: A field event in which the athlete tries to jump over (or clear) a horizontal crossbar set between two upright supports. The object is to clear the greatest height in the fewest attempts, with a maximum of three tries.

high-powered rifle: A big-bore military or big-game hunting rifle that shoots a bullet with a muzzle velocity of at least two thousand feet per second.

hill climb: An auto race up a hill, one car at a time, in a race against the clock.

hit for the cycle: Hitting a single, a double, a triple, and a home run in the same baseball game.

hitter: In volleyball, a player in position to spike or forcefully return the volleyball after being set up by the setter; or the player so designated by his or her immediate line position (front row or back row) on the court.

hole: Generally refers to a unit of the golf course that includes a tee, fairway, and green; used as in a nine-hole golf course or a four-par hole. *See also* cup.

home plate: The five-sided rubber slab set into the dirt at one corner of a baseball diamond. The pitcher throws toward it, the batter stands over it, and the base runner must cross it successfully to score a run.

home run: Any hit that enables the baseball or softball batter to round the bases and score a run in one continuous play. Home runs can be balls hit over the fence or balls that stay inside the park.

homestretch: On a race track, the length of track between the final turn and the finish line.

hook shot: A one-handed shot in which the body is turned sideways to the basket, the outside shooting arm is extended overhead, and the ball is released into an arc with a flick of the wrist. One of the hardest shots for a defender to block.

hop, step, and jump: *See* triple jump.

horizontal bar: A sturdy but pliant metal bar, about 1 inch in diameter, and about 8 feet long, horizontally positioned about 8 feet off the floor. It is used by the gymnast to execute swinging, looping and release-regrasp movements. A men's event.

hurdles: A sprint race that involves jumping over a series of metal or wooden obstacles (resembling gates) set up along the racetrack. The three types of hurdles races are the high, the intermediate, and the low hurdles, at distances of 100 meters (for women), 110 meters (for men), and 400 meters (for both men and women).

hypertrophy: A scientific term that essentially means larger and stronger muscles. Bodybuilders and weightlifters work to induce hypertrophy by overloading the exercised muscles, forcing them to lift more weight than they can normally handle. The result is increased strength and muscle mass.

I-formation: In football, an offensive setup that positions the fullback and the tailback in a line several yards directly behind the quarterback.

Iditarod Trail Sled Dog Race: A 1,158-mile sled dog racing endurance test. The Iditarod is an annual event that starts in Anchorage, Alaska, and ends in Nome. First held in 1973, it commemorates a well-known attempt in the winter of 1925 to rush emergency medicines and other supplies to Nome, which was fighting a diphtheria epidemic. The sport's longest and most prestigious event.

individual medley: An individual swimming race requiring that each leg (¼) of the race be completed using a different stroke, typically in the following order: butterfly, backstroke, breaststroke, and freestyle.

Indy car: A car that outwardly resembles a Formula One car but is several hundred pounds heavier, boosted for greater horsepower, and faster. These cars frequently reach speeds well above two hundred miles per hour on a straightaway. The only type of race cars allowed on the Championship Auto Racing Teams (CART) circuit, which includes the popular Indianapolis 500.

inning (badminton): The length of time that a player or a team holds service.

inning (baseball, softball): The unit into which a game is divided. There are nine innings in a regulation baseball game; there are seven innings in a men's and women's softball game.

innings (cricket): The unit into which a cricket match is divided. Matches are played in durations of one or two innings per team (each team has one or two innings to bat). As soon as ten of a team's eleven batsmen have been dismissed (put out), an innings is completed. Since an innings can continue for up to a full day, matches include breaks for meals and rest. Also means a turn at bat in a match, which for the batsman continues until he has been put out.

interception: In football, to catch and gain control over a pass thrown to an opposing player.

inward dive: In competitive diving, a maneuver in which the diver stands on the edge of the platform or springboard, facing away from the water, then springs backward but rotates forward.

2891

jab: A type of boxing punch that is a sharp, rapid snap of the arm, and which is thrown a short distance, often directly at the head or face.

jackknife: A forward dive performed by jumping off the springboard into the air, momentarily assuming a jackknife or pike pose (body bent at the waist and hands touching the ankles in a V-shape), then straightening the body so as to enter the water headfirst.

javelin throw: A field event that involves throwing the javelin for distance. The javelin is a long, tapered spear with a pointed tip. The men's javelin is about 8½ feet long; the women's javelin is a few inches over 7 feet.

jockey: A professional rider of race horses.

jump serve: A high-velocity volleyball serve in which the server strikes the ball after first taking a running jump from just behind the service line.

jump shot: Generally, a two-handed overhead shot in which the shooter releases the basketball at the top of the jump. Good rotation is imparted by a firm snap of the wrist.

jump ski: A waterskiing event that involves skiing up and over an inclined ramp.

kayak: A narrow, lightweight racing shell, the edges of which are tapered to a point at both the bow and the stern, and which is propelled through the water by a single long paddle with blades at either end. The top of the kayak is entirely covered except for the small cockpit reserved for the kayaker. More slender than a canoe.

kill: An unhittable or unreturnable attacking shot, such as in badminton, tennis, or volleyball, that scores the point for the hitter.

knockout: A victory scored by a boxer who is able to render his opponent unconscious or otherwise unable to continue the match. Following a knockdown, the fallen boxer has ten seconds to get back on his feet or the fight is declared over.

knuckleball: A baseball pitch thrown with little or no rotation, and which, as a result, moves around unpredictably as it approaches the plate.

lap: One complete trip around a race track or up and back the length of a pool.

lay-up: A shot in which the basketball is released near the rim and at the top of the jump, and frequently off the backboard. Lay-ups are often the end result of a drive to the basket.

leg: In a relay race, that length of the track or pool that each member of the team must complete in order to finish the race. In Olympic swimming and track and field, team relays consist of four legs, as does swimming's individual medley event.

light heavyweight (boxing): A weight classification in professional boxing with a 175-pound maximum limit. In amateur boxing, the maximum limit is 178 pounds.

light heavyweight (weightlifting): An international weight classification with a 181¾-pound maximum limit.

lightweight (boxing): A weight classification in professional boxing with a 135-pound maximum limit. In amateur boxing, the maximum limit is 132 pounds.

lightweight (judo): An international weight classification with a 156-pound maximum limit.

lightweight (weightlifting): An international weight classification with a 148¾-pound maximum limit.

line bowling: A style of bowling that involves rolling the ball along an imaginary line from the point of release to the target point.

line of scrimmage: The imaginary line parallel to the goal lines of a football field and extending the width of the field. It marks the position of the football and is reestablished as necessary after each gain or loss of yardage. From the offensive team's point of view, the line extends across the tip of the ball that points toward it. No player may cross the line until the ball is snapped (except for the center, whose fingers must cross the line in order to grip the ball).

lock: A wrestling hold that completely prevents the opponent from moving whichever part of his body is being held.

long-distance running: A footrace longer than one mile.

long-distance swimming: An open-water event longer than one mile.

long-horse vault: *See* vault.

long jump: A field event that involves sprinting toward a sand pit and jumping for distance.

luge: The French word for "sled." A small racing sled that seats one or two people. During competition, the luge athlete assumes the most aerodynamically efficient position possible, lying far back on the sled, head held up just enough to see the course. Steering is done by shifting the weight and manipulating the twin metal runners beneath the sled.

lunge: The classic fencing technique of attacking an opponent by stepping forward with the front foot (the foot on the same side of the body as the sword arm) while keeping the back foot planted and extending the sword arm.

mainsail: The principal sail on a ship having several sails.

majority decision: A victory scored by a boxer after two of the ring officials declare him the winner while the third official declares a draw.

man-to-man defense: In various team sports, a strategy in which each defensive player is assigned to guard an opposing player.

mandatory eight-count: A boxing rule specifying that once a knockdown occurs, the referee's count must automatically reach eight before the match can resume, if indeed it can resume. Used to allow the fallen boxer a few extra seconds to regain his composure before continuing the fight.

marathon: A footrace of twenty-six miles and three hundred eighty-five yards, run through public thoroughfares off-limits to traffic.

master: A title given to a martial artist who has achieved an advanced ranking after many years of study. *See also* belt.

match sprint: A 1,000-meter cycling race around a velodrome track. Only the last 200 meters are timed. During the first 800 meters, the cyclists try to position themselves for the final 200-meter rush to the finish line.

middle-distance running: A track event involving races whose length can be anywhere from eight hundred meters to one mile.

middleweight (boxing): A weight classification in professional boxing with a 160-pound limit. In amateur boxing, the limit is 165 pounds.

middleweight (judo): An international weight classification with a 189-pound maximum limit.

middleweight (weightlifting): An international weight classification with a 181$\frac{3}{4}$-pound maximum limit.

military press: In weightlifting, a lift made from a standing position and in which the barbell is pushed upward from shoulder level to an overhead position, and then lowered.

Mr./Ms. America: A U.S. amateur title awarded to the male and female champions in the Mr./Ms.

2893

America bodybuilding competition. Entrants compete for the title in three divisions, according to height: tall, medium, and short. Sanctioned by the Amateur Athletic Union.

Mr./Ms. Olympia: A world professional title awarded to the male and female champions in the Mr./Ms. Olympia bodybuilding competition. Entrants compete for the title in a number of weight classifications. Sanctioned by the International Federation of Bodybuilding.

Mr./Ms. Universe: A world amateur title awarded to the male and female champions in the Mr./Ms. Universe bodybuilding competition. Entrants compete for the title in a number of weight classifications. Sanctioned by the International Federation of Bodybuilding.

modified stock car: A standard assembly-line car whose power and efficiency have been boosted for greater performance, such as through improvements in the engine, the transmission, the suspension, and the fuel-injection system.

Most Valuable Player award: Any number of annual distinctions given to the most outstanding athletes in various team sports. The Most Valuable Players are usually those who have done the most to help their teams win games. Among the more popular sports, award recipients are often named at several levels of play within a particular sport: championship series, playoff series, and regular season. Generally speaking, the winning candidates (for the official league award) are determined by the votes of selected sports media associations.

motor-paced cycling: A cycling time trial in which a car or motorcycle is used to cut wind resistance for the cyclist, who rides just behind and very close to the vehicle in front in order to ride in the slipstream created by the vehicle. The reduced air resistance ensures the possibility of reaching higher speeds with less effort.

muscle mass: The relative size of a muscle, a muscle group, or of the physique as a whole. Along with clear definition and well-balanced proportion, muscle mass is a desirable quality among bodybuilders.

natatorium: A building that contains a swimming pool and facilities for holding aquatic competitions.

National Association for Stock Car Auto Racing (NASCAR): The title earned by the driver who accumulates the most points on the NASCAR circuit by the end of the racing season. Points are awarded according to how well the driver finishes in each officially sanctioned race.

National Basketball Association (NBA) Finals: The best-of-seven-games series that determines the season's NBA champions.

Nation's Cup: An international equestrian jumping competition for four-person teams.

Negro leagues: A series of professional leagues in the United States organized for black baseball players—largely, if not solely, the result of major league baseball's refusal to become integrated. The situation began to change in 1947, the year that Jackie Robinson, the major leagues' first black player, appeared in his first game for the Brooklyn Dodgers. By the late 1940's, the popularity of the Negro leagues had fallen as black players became absorbed into the newly integrated major leagues.

nelson: A wrestling hold that involves using the arms and hands to apply pressure to the opponent's head and upper arms. The quarter nelson, half nelson, and full nelson are variations of this type of hold.

Nordic skiing: Competitive events consisting of cross-country skiing and ski jumping.

offense: In various sports, the attempt to advance the ball or puck or to score points, runs, or goals against an opponent. Also, the specific game plan used by the team in possession of the ball (when it *has* the ball). A term used mostly in the context of certain team sports.

Olympic Games: The world's most elite international amateur sports exhibition, held every four years in a different host country and open to athletes from virtually every nation. Within the Olympic year, the Games are divided into two cycles, the Summer Olympics and the Winter Olympics (inaugurated in France in 1924). Beginning in 1994, however, the Summer and Winter Olympics will be held two years apart, with the Winter Games scheduled to occur that year. The Olympics were first held at Olympia in ancient Greece at four-year intervals from 776 B.C. to A.D. 393, when they were abolished by the Roman government. The earliest Games lasted only one day and consisted of a single footrace the length of the stadium. More sports, such as chariot racing, boxing, and the pentathlon, were eventually added, extending the festival (which also included religious celebrations) to seven days. The modern Games were resurrected in Athens, Greece, in 1896, mostly through the efforts of French educator and scholar Baron Pierre de Coubertin. His purpose was to revive the Greek tradition of a periodic sports festival and to promote international good will. In modern times, participating athletes engage in a great many different sports, almost from A to Z. Each Olympics may also include demonstration sports (the 1988 Games, for example, featured baseball and tennis). The Olympic Games are governed by the International Olympic Committee, headquartered in Lausanne, Switzerland.

Olympic lifting: The category of weightlifting events featured at the Olympic Games. Includes the clean and jerk and the snatch.

omnium: An event in track cycling that involves a series of races, each at distances ranging from one-quarter mile to two miles.

overhead smash: A tennis or badminton stroke that is hit from overhead with great force and power. Similar in motion to the serve. An effective put-away shot.

overtime: A period of extended play used when a game is tied at the end of regulation.

pairs: In figure skating competition, a program performed by two skaters, one male and one female, skating in tandem. The programs consist of dancing, jumps, turns, spins, lifts, and throws, among others. Set to music.

par: The number of strokes that an expert golfer would be expected to take to finish a hole or a course in ordinary weather conditions. Par for one hole is determined by allowing a certain number of strokes from the tee to the green (considering the distance between the two) and alloting two strokes for putting.

parallel bars: A gymnastics apparatus consisting of two parallel oval-shaped wooden or fiberglass poles approximately 11½ feet long and 5½ feet off the ground and set as far apart as the gymnast prefers. Used to perform routines that require balancing and swinging movements, for example. A men's event.

parry: A fencer's use of the sword to deflect an opponent's blade.

passing shot: In a tennis match, a ball that is hit past and outside the reach of an opponent who is positioned in the frontcourt or midcourt area.

peloton: A French word that means the "pack." The main group of cyclists in a race, typically near the front of the field of competitors.

penalty box: In ice hockey, a designated area off the ice in which a penalized player must wait for the penalty minutes to expire before being allowed to resume play. Until that time, that player's team will continue the game shorthanded. Penalizations create opportunities for power plays. *See also* power play.

pennant: The honor accorded to the winning team in both the National and the American League Championship Series. Both pennant champions advance to the World Series to decide major league baseball's overall season champion.

pentathlon: An Olympic competition involving five events. The modern Olympic pentathlon for men consists of fencing, pistol shooting, freestyle swimming, cross-country running, and horsemanship. The Olympic pentathlon for women was replaced by the heptathlon in 1984.

perfect game (baseball): A game in which the pitcher throws a shutout and allows no hits and no walks, and in which no opposing batter reaches first base under any circumstance.

perfect game (bowling): Scoring 300, the maximum number of points in a single game. A 300 game consists of twelve consecutive strikes.

pike: A position in which a diver or gymnast shapes his or her body like a V, with the body bent at the waist and the arms held straight out and to the sides or touching the feet or the backs of the knees, the legs are straight.

pin (bowling): One of the ten wooden figures that make up the target.

pin (golf): The metal upright flagstaff that indicates where the hole is.

pin (wrestling): Pushing the opponent's shoulder blades to the mat. In Olympic freestyle and Greco-Roman wrestling, the match is over (and won) the moment both blades are touching the mat.

pin bowling: A style of bowling that involves rolling the ball directly toward either a single pin or a specific pocket.

pistol: A handgun that can be aimed and fired with one hand.

pit stop: Leaving the auto raceway for an off-track area to change tires, refuel, or have repairs done.

pitch (baseball): A ball thrown from pitcher to batter.

pitch (golf): A shot that puts the ball onto the green from a point just off the green. Shorter shots of this type are called chip shots.

pitch (soccer): The playing field.

Pittsburgh Paint and Glass (PPG) Indy Car World Series Championship: The title earned by the auto racing driver who accumulates the most points on the Championship Auto Racing Teams (CART) circuit at the end of the racing season. Points are awarded according to how well the driver finishes in each officially sanctioned race.

platform diving: A competitive event involving dives off a fixed, nonflexible surface. The platform is set ten meters above the water in Olympic diving. Divers are judged on such elements as takeoff, execution, form, and entry. The degree of difficulty of each dive is also taken into account.

playoff: Generally, a series of games held at the end of the regular season to determine the finalists for a subsequent championship game or series (as in the Super Bowl or the World Series). "Play-off" may also mean a period of extended play when a game is tied after regulation play has ended, as in a sudden-death playoff in a golf match.

pocket (bowling): For a right-hander, the small space between the headpin (1-pin) and the 3-pin; for a left-hander, between the headpin and the 2-pin. The likelihood of rolling a strike is greatest at these target points. The ten bowling pins are assembled in the shape of a triangle. The topmost pin closest to the bowler is the headpin, or 1-pin. The very next row, left to right, includes the 2-pin and the 3-pin. then come the 4-, the 5-, and the 6-pins, and finally pins 7, 8 9, and 10.

2896

pocket (football): An area several yards behind the line of scrimmage in which the quarterback sets up to throw a pass. the pocket offers the quarterback the best possible pass protection. Once the ball is snapped, the pocket forms as the offensive line drops back to create this U-shaped barrier.

point: A unit of scoring in any game or contest.

point-of-aim: The point at which the archer sets the line of sight in order to calculate the best elevation for the flight of the arrow.

pole position: In auto racing, the innermost front-row position on the starting line. An advantage awarded to the driver with the fastest times in qualifying time trials held prior to the main racing event.

pole vault: A men's field event that involves using a long fiberglass or wooden pole to lift the body up and over a horizontally positioned crossbar set between two upright supports. The object is to clear (or go over) the crossbar at a height greater than the other competitors and in fewer tries.

pommel horse: A men's event that involves performing any number of balancing and swinging gymnastics moves, while moving back and forth across the top the horse, using both the pommels and the top of the horse and not letting one's legs touch the horse. The horse is a rectangular apparatus approximately five feet long and one foot wide and covered with padded leather. Two pommels, or handles, are set on top and parallel to each other. Also called a side horse.

post: An offensive position occupied by a basketball player just outside the lane, either down close to the basket (the low post) or up around the free throw line (the high post).

post up: On offense in basketball, to set up in a low-post position in order to gain a scoring advantage against a shorter basketball player or an opponent who is in foul trouble.

power lifting: A category of weightlifting competition involving the bench press, the dead lift, and the squat. Both men and women are allowed to participate in a variety of weight classes. Not an Olympic category. *See also* Olympic lifting.

power play: A situation in a hockey game in which one team outnumbers the other on the ice because of players in the penalty box. The first team's numerical advantage generally means greater scoring opportunities against a shorthanded team. Often the team with the advantage will send its fastest skaters and best scorers into the game in an effort to overwhelm the opponent.

press: A defensive strategy in basketball that involves applying intense man-to-man pressure against the opposing team from the moment the ball is inbounded (full-court press) or just after the ball crosses the half-court line (half-court press).

professional: Generally, one who competes for prize money or who is paid to play.

Professional Rodeo Cowboys Association (PRCA) World Champion All-Around Cowboy: The title earned by the cowboy who wins the most money on the PRCA rodeo circuit in a single year. The most prestigious distinction in professional rodeo.

pull: To ride at the front of a group of cyclists, where the wind resistance is greatest and where the lead cyclist is without the benefit of a slipstream. Instead, the leader creates the drafting effect for the others. The members of a cycling team are expected to take turns pulling the others during a race in order to allow every member a chance to conserve energy yet maintain speed.

pumping iron: A slang phrase that means exercising with weights (such as barbells and dumbbells).

pursuit: A track cycling event in which individuals or teams of riders start the race at opposite ends of the track and try to catch up to the opposing side.

put-away: Similar to a kill shot, an unhittable or unreturnable shot that scores a point for the hitter in volleyball, tennis, or badminton.

putt: A golf stroke made with the ball on the green.

putting green: *See* green.

qualifying: For an individual athlete or a team of athletes, that act of becoming eligible for a particular game or tournament by fulfilling certain requirements. Qualifying can arise through a variety of ways, such as through preliminary heats or through individual statistics or through team win-loss records.

racing shell: A lightweight and usually very narrow racing boat pulled by oars.

randori: A Japanese word that means "free exercise." Judo sparring sessions designed to develop strength, speed, stamina, and technique.

rangefinder: An archer's device that helps in estimating the distance to the target or in locating the point-of-aim.

reading the green: Setting up a golf putt by first studying closely the slope and the surface of the green.

rebound (basketball): An unsuccessful shot that caroms off the backboard or the rim: or the act of gaining possession of such a shot attempt.

rebound (ice hockey): A pass or a shot attempt that caroms off the boards encompassing the ice; or the act of gaining possession of such a pass or shot attempt.

referee's decision: A victory scored by a boxer who has been declared the winner by the referee while the two ring judges have each declared a draw.

regatta: A series of races involving rowboats, sailboats, or speedboats.

relay: A team race, such as in swimming and track events, that requires each team member to complete one leg (of which there are usually four) of the race, one competitor at a time. In swimming, a leg is complete as each swimmer touches the wall. In track, this occurs when the baton is passed from one runner to another (except on the final leg).

reverse dive: A maneuver in which the diver faces the water, jumps up off the board, rotates backward, and enters the water headfirst, facing the board, or feetfirst, facing away from the board.

rhythmic gymnastics: An international and Olympic (as of 1984) category of events for female gymnasts, who compete according to rules prescribed by the International Gymnastics Federation (IGF). In individual competition, the gymnasts perform choreographed routines using one of the following objects in each routine: a ribbon, a hoop, a ball, a rope, or clubs. Every two years, the IGF selects four of the five apparatus to be used in routines for the next two years. The routines are performed on a 40-foot-by-40-foot floor area, are set to music, last 60 to 90 seconds, and the gymnast and apparatus must be moving at all times. Although not yet an Olympic event, group competition consists of synchronized routines performed by six gymnasts at once.

rifle: A shoulder weapon with a stock and a long barrel with spiral grooves cut into the inside, and which shoots a bullet.

rings: *See* stationary rings.

round (boxing): The three-minute periods into which a boxing match is divided. A one-minute rest period separates each round. The number of rounds in a match depends on whether the event is amateur or professional.

round (golf): The eighteen holes of a golf course. May also simply mean a game of golf; to play a "round" of golf is to play a game of eighteen holes.

routine: A set of graceful movements, difficult stunts, or other elements or tricks performed on a gymnastics apparatus or in floor exercises.

run (baseball): A point scored whenever an offensive player successfully crosses home plate.

run (bobsledding, skiing): The inclined course traversed by the participant.

run (cricket): A point scored whenever the two batsmen successfully exchange wickets (run from one wicket to the other) during a play.

run batted in (RBI): In baseball and softball, a statistic credited to a batter who gets a hit and causes a base runner to score a run. Even if the batter flies out or is thrown out on the play, the run will count unless the third out results. A batter can also be credited with an RBI by being walked by the pitcher and forcing home the runner.

rush: The act of advancing the football by running with it on a play from scrimmage. Also, the defense's attempt to penetrate the offensive backfield in order to get to the ball.

Ryder Cup: A series of men's golf tournaments between professional teams from the United States and various European countries. Begun in 1927 by British businessman Samuel Ryder for competition between professional golfers from the United States and Great Britain. Held every odd-numbered year.

sabre fencing: One of the three styles of fencing. A sabre is a sword with a curved guard protecting the back of the hand and a fairly rigid blade with a blunted tip. A cutting and thrusting weapon. *See also* épée fencing, foil fencing.

sack: A statistic credited to a defender who manages to tackle the quarterback behind the line of scrimmage in a football game.

saddle bronc riding: A rodeo competition that involves riding a saddled wild, bucking horse for eight seconds using one hand to grip a strap attached to the saddle. Riders are judged on how well they ride and how hard the horse bucks. Rodeo's classic event has its roots in the Old West, when restless ranch hands would compete to see who was the best at riding wild horses.

sail: A large, billowing expanse of fabric, such as cotton or polyester, used on ships to harness the wind and propel the ship forward.

Salchow: A figure skating maneuver achieved by jumping from the back inside edge of one skate, turning once in the air, and landing on the back outside edge of the second skate. Named for its inventor, the Swedish skater Ulrich Salchow, who in 1908 won the first gold medal ever given in men's Olympic figure skating.

sand trap: A depression filled with loose sand and usually set near the green on a golf course.

save (baseball): A statistic credited to a relief pitcher who enters the game with his team ahead and preserves the victory. To earn the save, the reliever must generally come into a situation where the reliever faces the potentially tying run and must protect a lead of from one to three runs. On the other hand, a reliever who enters the game with the team behind or tied but pitches a victory will be credited with a win.

save (ice hockey): A statistic credited to a goalie who deflects a shot on goal or otherwise prevents a goal from being scored.

school figures: *See* compulsory figures.

schooner: A fore-and-aft rigged ship equipped with two or more masts. Rigging refers to the lines of rope stretching from the tops of the masts to the deck and which are used for support.

2899

schussing: Skiing at high speed straight down the mountain's natural slope—the steepest and fastest line of descent.

scissors volley: A soccer maneuver that involves leaping up and, from a horizontal position, kicking the ball using a scissorslike leg motion.

screwball: A reverse curveball. A baseball pitch that veers or breaks in the direction opposite that of a curveball. A screwball thrown by a right-handed pitcher will break down and toward a right-handed batter.

sculls: A rowing sport in which two oars mounted in fixed positions on either side of the racing shell are pulled at the same time to propel the boat in one direction.

sensei: A Japanese word meaning "teacher" or "instructor." A title accorded to instructors in the martial arts such as judo.

serve and volley player: A tennis player whose game strategy is to rush the net aggressively after serving the ball, anticipating the volley or the put-away.

setter: The volleyball player who occupies the middle front row position. He or she must put the ball up into the air near the net so that the hitter can spike it.

shoot the tube: To ride a surfboard into the hollow tunnel of water created by the curl of an ocean wave.

shot put: A field event that involves heaving the shot for distance. A shot is an iron or brass ball weighing from eight to sixteen pounds (sixteen in Olympic competition).

shotgun formation: In football, an offensive formation used to give the quarterback more time to pass. The quarterback lines up several yards behind the center, while the running backs position themselves farther out as flankers or blockers.

show jumping: An equestrian event in which horse and rider attempt to jump over a succession of fences at varying distances within a prescribed time limit. Held in an arena.

shutout: A statistic credited to a baseball or softball pitcher who does not allow the opposition to score any runs in a game. More generally, a shutout occurs when one team fails to score a point in any sporting event.

shuttlecock: The lightweight, conical object volleyed back and forth in badminton.

side-horse vault: *See* vault.

sidehorse: *See* pommel horse.

single: In baseball or softball, a hit that allows the batter to reach first base.

single wing: In football, an offensive formation with an emphatic strong side (the side that has more players lined up either left or right of the center, thus making that side "stronger"). In the single wing, the tailback lines up about four to five yards directly behind the center and receives the snap. On the strong side, the fullback lines up about a yard ahead of and just to the side of the tailback, and can also receive the snap. The quarterback positions himself as a blocking back a few yards away from the center, again on the strong side. The fourth back, the wingback, lines up behind and just outside the offensive end on the strong side.

sit-ski: A much-wider-than-normal water ski with a seat affixed to the top. Invented especially for disabled athletes who are paralyzed from the waist down.

ski jumping: A competitive distance event that involves gliding straight down an upward curling ramp or hill without help from ski poles, taking off into air, and trying to achieve the greatest distance possible before landing. A event in Nordic skiing, which also includes cross-country skiing.

skipper: The person in charge of a ship.

2900

sky hook: A high-arching hook shot taken from far above the rim of a basketball hoop. Popularized by former NBA star Kareem Abdul-Jabbar, for whom the phrase was coined.

slalom (skiing): A race that involves negotiating as fast as possible the downhill zigzag pattern of the course. This design forces the skier to execute a number of turns through gates set up at different distances and angles. A race against the clock. An event in the Alpine skiing category, which also includes downhill, giant slalom, and super giant slalom ski racing.

slalom (waterskiing): An event that involves zigzagging through a line of buoys set out lengthwise across the water. One of three basic water skiing events, the others being jump skiing and trick riding.

slam dunk: An especially forceful and intimidating basketball scoring move in which the ball is stuffed or pushed through the rim rather than shot.

slap shot: A high-velocity hockey shot in which the shooter takes the hockey stick all the way back for increased power and then propels the puck at speeds that are often well above one hundred miles per hour.

slider: A baseball pitch that is thrown like a fastball but moves like a curveball, except that it breaks slightly later than a curve, just as it crosses the plate.

slingshotting: A maneuver in auto racing and cycling in which the slipstreaming car or cyclist uses the power and energy conserved to shoot past the lead racer.

slipstreaming: Riding in the slipstream, the pocket of reduced air resistance and forward suction behind a rapidly moving object, such as a lead race car, a lead cyclist, or a motorcycle, in order to conserve energy while maintaining speed. *See also* drafting.

slugging percentage: A statistical category that indicates a baseball batter's ability to get extra-base hits (doubles, triples, and home runs) with teammates in scoring position. Figured by dividing the total number of bases reached safely on hits by the total number of at-bats.

small-bore: In shooting sports, a term that refers to small-caliber firearms, in the .22 range.

snatch: In weightlifting, a lift performed by pulling the barbell off the floor and in one continuous motion bringing it to rest in an overhead position.

somersault: A maneuver in which the body is turned one full revolution, either forward or backward. The head and feet rotate up and over each other. Frequently used in diving and gymnastics. Often called a "flip" when executed completely in the air.

spare: In bowling, the feat of knocking down all ten pins with both balls in a single frame.

spike: To hit the volleyball downward into the opposite court with as much velocity as possible. The spiker often tries to jump high up over the net because the added height creates a better hitting angle.

spitball: A baseball pitch that moves unpredictably, the result of spit, sweat, petroleum jelly, or some other substance having been applied to the ball. Illegal since the 1920's.

split decision: A victory scored by a boxer after two of the ring officials declare him the winner while the third official votes for his opponent.

split-fingered fastball: A baseball pitch thrown with the same arm motion and speed as a fastball but with the index and middle fingers spread more widely apart. The ball tends to dip sharply just as it reaches the plate.

spot bowling: A style of bowling that involves rolling the ball across a specific marker—such as one of the seven triangular arrows set into the line just beyond the foul line—as the target point for releasing the ball.

2901

spread eagle: One of the basic movements of free skating, in which the skater performs smooth glides through large circles or straight lines. To do this, both skates must be turned outward from each other in a line (right toes pointing directly right, left toes point directly left) and the heels spread apart a little more than hip distance.

springboard diving: A competitive event involving dives off a springboard. A springboard is a flat and flexible board mounted at one end and positioned over a fulcrum. The diver uses the board as a launching pad, attaining the height necessary to perform the dive. Olympic competition consists of the one-meter and three-meter dives (the springboards are set one and three meters above the water). Divers are judged on such elements as takeoff, execution, form, and entry. The degree of difficulty of each dive is also taken into account.

sprint: An all-out race to the finish line. Sprint events occur in such sports as cycling, speed skating, and track and field.

squat: A weightlifting exercise or a competitive event that involves balancing the barbell behind the head and atop the shoulders, then squatting down and rising to a standing position.

stage race: A cycling race divided into a succession of individual stages or segments. Each stage is really only a shorter race, and the distance of each race will vary, sometimes greatly. The cyclist who wins the entire race is the one with the lowest overall time after his or her times for all the stages are added together. The Tour de France is the world's longest and most famous stage race.

Stanley Cup Playoffs: The end-of-season series of games used to determine the National Hockey League champion team. The preliminary rounds lead up to final best-of-seven-games Stanley Cup Championship Series between the Wales and the Campbell Conference champions.

stationary rings: A men's gymnastics event performed while hanging from two rings suspended from above by long straps. Each ring is approximately 7½ inches in diameter and positioned about 8 feet off the floor. Routines on the rings combine swinging, balancing movements such as handstands and crosses (where the body is held vertically and the arms are fully extended in the shape of a cross) and are a test of strength and stamina. In competition, the rings should remain stationary.

steeplechase (horse racing): An event that takes place on a steeplechase course consisting of obstacles such as fences, water jumps, and open ditches.

steeplechase (track and field): A race in which the competitors encounter a series of hurdles and water jumps. The men's Olympic steeplechase is 3,000 meters long.

stern: The back of a ship or boat.

steroids: A class of natural and artificial organic chemical substances with significant applications in medicine, biology, and chemistry. Various types of artificial steroids are used therapeutically for such reasons as fighting inflammation of tissues or stimulating physical growth. Anabolic steroids are synthetically derived from the male hormone testosterone. They have often been taken by athletes in training to build up the size of their muscles or to help their injuries heal faster. Because of the dangerous side effects associated with using steroids, however, many of the organizations and national governing bodies that regulate various worldwide sports have banned them, imposing suspensions, fines, or other penalties if their use is detected during drug testing. Drug testing has become common at a number of international sporting events such as the Olympic Games and the World Championships.

stock car: Technically speaking, an unmodified race car that resembles its standard assembly-line model. In actuality, however, the likeness ends with the visible similarities. For the purposes of

2902

competition, stock cars are always modified to some degree to ensure peak performance. Alterations are often made to the engine and other critical components—whatever will make the car go faster.

strike (baseball): A pitch that the batter swings at but misses, or hits into foul territory for strikes one or two, or lets pass through the strike zone without swinging (a called strike). Three strikes and the batter is out.

strike (bowling): Knocking down all ten pins on the first roll in a single frame.

strikeout: A statistic credited to a pitcher every time a batter is retired solely on strikes. Credited also to the batter.

striker: On a soccer team, the offensive player who occupies the central forward position and who has a major responsibility to score goals.

stroke (golf): The unit of scoring in golf, one stroke being charged to a player for each shot taken, including penalty strokes. Or the controlled swing used to hit the ball.

stroke (rowing): The crew member who sits in the rear of the racing shell and who is responsible for setting the rowing pace for the oarsmen. Or this crew member's act of setting the pace ("setting the stroke"). Also, the rower's use of an oar to pull the shell through the water.

stroke (swimming): Any of several popular swimming styles involving the arms, hands, and feet. Also, the swimmer's controlled use of the arms and legs to move through the water.

stroke (tennis): Any of several popular methods of hitting the ball, such as the forehand and the backhand. Also, the controlled swing used to hit the ball.

sudden-death overtime: A method for determining the winner of a game still tied at the end of regulation play. Ordinarily, the first player or team to score a numerical advantage wins. In professional football, for example, the team that scores first in the fifteen-minute overtime period wins the game.

Super Bowl: The yearly postseason January spectacle between the champions of the National Football Conference and the American Football Conference of the National Football League (NFL). The game that decides the overall NFL champion.

super heavyweight (boxing): A weight classification in Olympic (amateur) boxing for athletes weighing more than 200 pounds.

super heavyweight (weightlifting): An international weight classification for athletes weighing more than 242 pounds.

super set: In weightlifting sports, a set of exercises for one group of muscles that is performed just before a set for an opposing muscle group, followed by a normal rest interval.

swan dive: A front dive in which the body is fully extended, the back is arched, the arms are outstretched, and the entry into the water is head first.

sweeper: On a soccer team, a defensive player who is free to roam in front of or behind his or her team's rear defensive line.

T-formation: An early offensive formation in football, which has been modified several times over the years, that positions the backfield players into roughly the shape of a T. The quarterback lines up directly over the center, the fullback sets up several yards right behind the quarterback, and the two halfbacks position themselves on either side and slightly ahead of the fullback. The modern T, or pro set, removes the third halfback. Another variation, the split T, removes the middle back and spreads the offensive linemen a little farther apart along the line of scrimmage.

2903

take a wicket: In cricket, the act of putting out the batsman by throwing the ball at the wicket and dislodging at least one of the bails.

takedown: Controlling an opponent and forcing him to the wrestling mat.

target archery: Shooting at targets placed at varying distances.

technical foul: A basketball rules violation that arises principally in the instance of flagrant and unsportsmanlike conduct on or off the court and before or after play has stopped. Such behavior is most often directed at an opponent or a referee. The nonoffending team can be awarded free throws and possession of the ball.

technical knockout: A victory scored by a boxer after the referee has stopped the match because the other boxer cannot continue fighting or cannot really defend himself, or because that boxer has indicated that he wants to stop.

test match cricket: An international first-class match in which the best players from one country team up to compete against similar players from other countries. Test matches often take as long as five days to complete the required two innings per team.

thoroughbreds: Race horses bred for speed and stamina. Descended from Arabian stallions that were brought over to England between 1690 and 1730 and crossed with English racing mares. These sensitive, spirited animals have delicate heads, slender bodies, and long muscles and legs.

time trial: A form of cycling competition in which riders start the race at intervals of several minutes apart from each other. The cyclist with the best time wins.

toe loop jump: A skating maneuver achieved by jumping off the back outside edge of one skate after having planted the toe of the other skate into the ice (to assist takeoff), turning once in the air, and landing on the outside edge of the first skate.

top fuel: A category of professional drag racing called the top fuel eliminators, featuring dragsters that burn a potent blend of methanol and nitromethane fuel. Top fuel vehicles are of two types—funny cars and top fuel dragsters—and are the most powerful piston-driven machines in the world. The driver relies primarily on a hand-activated parachute to stop the car, a process that can take as much as twelve hundred feet. Top fuel competition involves a series of elimination heats, two cars per heat. These cars are built with a lightweight tubular frame, wide rear tires, and a powerful engine placed front (funny cars) or back (top fuel dragsters) of the frame; they often reach speeds in the range of 290 miles per hour over the one-quarter-mile course. *See also* funny car.

topspin: The forward rotation of a tennis ball imparted by sweeping the racket face up and over the ball at the point of contact.

touchdown: In football, a scoring play of six points that are earned by successfully advancing the football across the opposing goal line and into the end zone. Passing, rushing, and recovering a fumble are various ways of scoring a touchdown.

tours: The most important and usually the longest stage races of the international cycling season. A tour is won by completing all of the stages in the shortest amount of time. The most famous of these is the approximately 2,200-mile-long Tour de France.

track events: In men's Olympic competition, these include the 100-, 200-, and 400-meter dashes, the 800- and 1,500-meter runs, and 5- and 10-kilometer runs, walking races of 20 and 50 kilometers, the 110- and 400-meter hurdles, the 3,000-meter steeplechase, the 4 x 100- and 4 x 400-meter relays, and the marathon. On the women's side, these include the 100-, 200-, and 400-meter dashes, the 800- and 1,500-meter runs, the 3- and 10-kilometer runs, the 100- and 400-meter hurdles, the 4 x 100- and 4 x 400-meter relays, and the marathon.

2904

trampoline: A gymnastics apparatus in which a rectangular canvas cover or webbing is attached by springs to a surrounding metal frame. The trampoline's canvas cover normally stands about three to four feet above the ground. Used to perform a variety of jumping, somersaulting, and other acrobatic elements. Not a standard event in artistic gymnastic competitions.

trim: To adjust the sails of a ship in order to keep the ship on course.

triple: In baseball or softball, a hit that allows the batter to reach third base.

triple bogey: Finishing a golf hole at three strokes over par for that hole.

Triple Crown: Generally speaking, those events or tournaments in a particular sport that are considered to be the three major ones; or the feat of winning all three of them in a single season or year.

Triple Crown (baseball): The unofficial championship title awarded to the major league baseball players who at the end of the regular season lead their leagues (National and American) in home runs, batting average, and runs batted in.

Triple Crown (horse racing): The unofficial championship title awarded to the horse that wins the Kentucky Derby, the Preakness Stakes, and the Belmont Stakes in the same season.

triple jump: A field event that is similar to the long jump in that it involves jumping for distance. The mechanics, however, differ greatly. The triple jumper is allowed to take three sequential jumps following a running start. The first landing is made on the takeoff foot, the second landing on the other foot, and the third and final landing on both feet. Also called the hop, step, and jump after the three basic movements required.

tuck: A diving and gymnastic position in which the knees are bent, the thighs are held tightly against the chest, and the hands are wrapped around the lower legs.

tumbling: A gymnastics event performed down a large floor mat and in which the gymnast executes handsprings, twists, rolls, somersaults, and other acrobatic moves in a continuous series. Not a standard event in artistic gymnastic competitions.

twist: A dive that requires twisting the body sideways, in a half-twist, a full-twist, or more before entering the water. In gymnastics, twists are added to flips to increase the difficulty of the trick.

Uber Cup: A trophy awarded in women's international badminton play. It goes to the winner of the Ladies International Badminton Championship, held every three years.

unanimous decision: A victory scored by a boxer after all three of the ring officials (the two ring judges and the referee) have declared him the winner.

uneven parallel bars: A women's gymnastics event in which the gymnast performs a variety of continuous swinging and balancing tricks, moving between and around both bars. The apparatus consists of two wooden or fiberglass rails affixed to metal supports and set at different heights. The bars are parallel to each other and, in competition, are set at 7½ feet and 5 feet off the floor.

vault: A gymnastics event that involves vaulting over a padded, rectangular, leather covered apparatus a little more than 5 feet 1 inch long, slightly more than one foot wide, and raised about 4½ feet high for men and 3½ feet high for women, called a horse. Gymnasts start by running toward the horse, then jump off a springboard, place their hands on the horse, and shove off, landing feet first on the other side. While in the air either before or after hitting the horse, the gymnast often performs acrobatic somersaults or other movements that raise his or her score. Men vault over the horse lengthwise, from end to end (also called long-horse vault), and women vault over the side, widthwise (also called side-horse vault).

velodrome: A cycling racetrack with banked turns and usually made of wood or concrete.

Vezina Trophy: A yearly honor won by the National Hockey League's top goaltender, as determined by the league's general managers.

victory lap: The extra lap taken by the winning driver, cyclist, or runner once the race is over. A gesture of celebration between athlete and spectator.

volley: In badminton, tennis, or volleyball, to hit the shuttlecock or the ball while it is airborne and before it has touched the court; or hitting the ball back and forth in continuous play.

walk: A statistic credited to a baseball or softball pitcher for throwing four "balls"—pitches outside the strike zone—thereby sending the batter to first base. Credited also to the batter.

water hazard: Any body of standing water, such as a lake, a pond, or a stream, set within the boundaries of the golf course. Does not include "casual water," water that accumulates on the course such as from rain.

welterweight: A weight classification in professional and amateur boxing with a 147-pound maximum limit.

white-water racing: A race, or that portion of a race, that takes place through the white water, or the rapids, of a river or waterway.

wicket: In cricket, one of the two frames consisting of three wooden stumps, each twenty-eight inches high, atop which are set two bails. The bowler hurls the ball at the wicket and tries to dislodge the bails. If that happens, the batsman is out. Also refers to a batsman's turn at bat during an innings.

Wightman Cup: A yearly tennis tournament between women players from the United States and Great Britain.

Wimbledon: The oldest and most highly regarded international tennis event in the world. This annual grand slam tournament is officially called "The Lawn Tennis Championships" at the All-England Club in Church Road, Wimbledon, England.

wind-aided time: In certain track events, a performance time that has been assisted favorably by wind blowing generally in the direction of the race or finish line at a predetermined velocity. Wind-aided times are not counted as official records because of the advantage that is said to have occurred. The International Amateur Athletic Federation, which governs track and field, does not recognize as world or national records times in sprints and horizontal jumps set with a tailwind in excess of 2.0 meters per second.

windmill delivery: A softball pitching delivery that requires rapidly rotating the pitching arm in a circular underhand direction. A windmill windup allows the pitcher to generate as much velocity as possible prior to releasing the ball. The cricket bowler also uses a windmill-style delivery, but in an overhand direction.

Winner's Circle: A section away from a racetrack's finish line where the winning jockey and horse are officially awarded.

World Championship of Beach Volleyball: The annual fall beach volleyball tournament between the best two-person teams. Sponsored by the Association of Volleyball Professionals.

World Championship of Drivers: The title earned by the driver who accumulates the most points on the Formula One (Grand Prix) circuit during the racing season. Points are awarded according to how well the driver finishes in each race.

World Cup (golf): A yearly international four-day tournament in which thirty-two two-person teams from more than fifty countries compete in stroke play matches.

World Cup (skiing): An annual series of international Alpine skiing events for amateurs. The World Cup is awarded to the male and female winners.

World Cup (soccer): One of the most popular events in any sport. Soccer's World Cup tournament features the best teams from twenty-four countries. It is held every four years.

World Series: The championship best-of-seven-games baseball series between the pennant winners from the National League and the American League played each October. Determines major league baseball's overall season champion. Originated in 1903, when the National League's Pittsburgh Pirates played the American League's Boston Red Sox in a best-of-nine-games series. Boston won, five games to three.

wrist shot: An ice hockey shot delivered with a quick snap of the wrists. The shooter uses the blade of the hockey stick to flip the puck toward the goal. Unlike the faster, more powerful slap shot, no backswing is involved.

zone defense (basketball): A defensive strategy in which each player is assigned to a specified zone or area around the basket being defended, and must therefore guard any opposing player who invades that zone. Almost the opposite of the man-to-man defense, in which each defender must guard a specific opponent.

zone defense (football): The same idea as in basketball's zone defense. Each member of the defensive secondary, and often each of the linebackers, must defend a specified zone on the field and cover any opposing player who invades that zone.

Born	Name	Sport	Country
March 29, 1867	Cy Young	Baseball	United States
April 2, 1867	Eugen Sandow	Bodybuilding	Germany, England
May 9, 1870	Harry Vardon	Golf	England
March 3, 1872	Willie Keeler	Baseball	United States
October 14, 1873	Ray Ewry	High jump, Long jump, Triple jump	United States
February 24, 1874	Honus Wagner	Baseball	United States
September 5, 1874	Nap Lajoie	Baseball	United States
October 13, 1876	Rube Waddell	Baseball	United States
September 9, 1877	Frank Chance	Baseball	United States
January 1, 1878	Bobby Walthour	Cycling	United States
January 29, 1878	Barney Oldfield	Auto racing	United States
March 31, 1878	Jack Johnson	Boxing	United States
November 26, 1878	Major Taylor	Cycling	United States
May, 1880	Willie Anderson	Golf	Scotland, United States
August 12, 1880	Christy Mathewson	Baseball	United States
July 21, 1881	Johnny Evers	Baseball	United States
May 5, 1883	Chief Bender	Baseball	United States
December 18, 1886	Ty Cobb	Baseball	United States
December 20, 1886	Hazel Wightman	Tennis	United States
February 26, 1887	Grover Alexander	Baseball	United States
July 16, 1887	Shoeless Joe Jackson	Baseball	United States
November 6, 1887	Walter Johnson	Baseball	United States
April 4, 1888	Tris Speaker	Baseball	United States
May 28, 1888	Jim Thorpe	Football, Baseball, Decathlon, Pentathlon, High jump, Broad jump	United States
July 22, 1888	Floretta Doty McCutcheon	Bowling	United States
July 13, 1889	Stan Coveleski	Baseball	United States
October 4, 1889	John Kelly, Sr.	Rowing	United States
October 9, 1889	Rube Marquard	Baseball	United States
July 30, 1890	Casey Stengel	Baseball	United States
August 26, 1890	Duke Kahanamoku	Swimming, Surfing	United States
March 4, 1891	Dazzy Vance	Baseball	United States
December 21, 1892	Walter Hagen	Golf	United States
February 10, 1893	Bill Tilden	Tennis	United States
March 24, 1893	George Sisler	Baseball	United States
May 8, 1893	Francis D. Ouimet	Golf	United States
August 18, 1893	Burleigh Grimes	Baseball	United States
June 9, 1894	Nedo Nadi	Fencing	Italy
February 6, 1895	Babe Ruth	Baseball	United States
June 24, 1895	Jack Dempsey	Boxing	United States
September 24, 1895	Tommy Armour	Golf	Scotland

GREAT ATHLETES

Born	Name	Sport	Country
April 27, 1896	Rogers Hornsby	Baseball	United States
April 26, 1897	Eddie Eagan	Boxing, Bobsledding	United States
June 13, 1897	Paavo Nurmi	Long-distance runs, Steeplechase	Finland
May 25, 1898	Gene Tunney	Boxing	United States
August 13, 1898	Jean Borotra	Tennis	France
October 30, 1898	Bill Terry	Baseball	United States
May 24, 1899	Suzanne Lenglen	Tennis	France
November 11, 1899	Pie Traynor	Baseball	United States
December 15, 1899	Harold Abrahams	Sprints, Long jump	England
January 18, 1900	George Charles Calnan	Fencing	United States
March 6, 1900	Lefty Grove	Baseball	United States
March 8, 1900	Anne Barton Townsend	Field hockey	United States
April 12, 1900	Joe Lapchick	Basketball	United States
April 26, 1900	Hack Wilson	Baseball	United States
May 9, 1900	Bob Askin	Rodeo	United States
August 11, 1900	Charles Paddock	Sprints	United States
October 20, 1900	Judy Johnson	Baseball	United States
December 20, 1900	Gabby Hartnett	Baseball	United States
April 1, 1901	Johnny Farrell	Golf	United States
September 21, 1901	Learie Constantine	Cricket	Trinidad, England
December 14, 1901	Henri Cochet	Tennis	France
January 16, 1902	Eric Liddell	Sprints	Scotland
February 27, 1902	Ethelda Bleibtrey	Swimming	United States
February 27, 1902	Gene Sarazen	Golf	United States
March 17, 1902	Bobby Jones	Golf	United States
April 6, 1903	Mickey Cochrane	Baseball	United States
May 11, 1903	Charlie Gehringer	Baseball	United States
May 17, 1903	James "Cool Papa" Bell	Baseball	United States
May 22, 1903	Al Simmons	Baseball	United States
June 11, 1903	Ernie Nevers	Football	United States
June 13, 1903	Red Grange	Football	United States
June 19, 1903	Lou Gehrig	Baseball	United States
June 20, 1903	Glenna Collett Vare	Golf	United States
June 22, 1903	Carl Hubbell	Baseball	United States
July 3, 1903	Irvine "Ace" Bailey	Ice hockey	Canada
June 2, 1904	Johnny Weissmuller	Swimming	United States
May 3, 1905	Red Ruffing	Baseball	United States
July 2, 1905	René Lacoste	Tennis	France
September 28, 1905	Max Schmeling	Boxing	Germany
October 6, 1905	Helen Wills Moody	Tennis	United States
July 7, 1906	Satchel Paige	Baseball	United States
October 11, 1906	Dutch Clark	Football	United States
February 14, 1907	Johnny Longden	Horse racing	Canada
September 8, 1907	Buck Leonard	Baseball	United States
October 22, 1907	Jimmie Foxx	Baseball	United States
October 23, 1907	Gertrude Ederle	Swimming	United States
January 20, 1908	Martha Norelius	Swimming	United States
February 17, 1908	Buster Crabbe	Swimming	United States
August 20, 1908	Al Lopez	Baseball	United States
August 27, 1908	Donald G. Bradman	Cricket	Australia

Born	Name	Sport	Country
September 29, 1908	Eddie Tolan	Sprints	United States
November 3, 1908	Bronko Nagurski	Football	United States
November 26, 1908	Lefty Gomez	Baseball	United States
February 11, 1909	Max Baer	Boxing	United States
March 2, 1909	Mel Ott	Baseball	United States
April 2, 1909	Luke Appling	Baseball	United States
May 18, 1909	Fred Perry	Tennis	England
May 25, 1910	Jimmy Demaret	Golf	United States
June 23, 1910	Lawson Little	Golf	United States
October 14, 1910	John Wooden	Basketball	United States
January 1, 1911	Hank Greenberg	Baseball	United States
January 16, 1911	Dizzy Dean	Baseball	United States
November 24, 1911	Joe Medwick	Baseball	United States
December 21, 1911	Josh Gibson	Baseball	United States
February 4, 1912	Byron Nelson	Golf	United States
April 8, 1912	Sonja Henie	Figure skating	Norway
May 27, 1912	Sam Snead	Golf	United States
June 5, 1912	Lee Petty	Auto racing	United States
August 13, 1912	Ben Hogan	Golf	United States
December 12, 1912	Henry Armstrong	Boxing	United States
January 7, 1913	Johnny Mize	Baseball	United States
January 13, 1913	Don Hutson	Football	United States
September 12, 1913	Jesse Owens	Sprints, Long jump	United States
September 28, 1913	Alice Marble	Tennis	United States
December 13, 1913	Archie Moore	Boxing	United States
March 17, 1914	Sammy Baugh	Football	United States
May 13, 1914	Joe Louis	Boxing	United States
June 26, 1914	Babe Didrikson Zaharias	Hurdles, Long jump, High jump, Shot put, Javelin throw, Golf, Basketball, Softball	United States
August 1, 1914	Lloyd Mangrum	Golf	United States
October 30, 1914	Marion Ladewig	Bowling	United States
November 25, 1914	Joe DiMaggio	Baseball	United States
February 1, 1915	Sir Stanley Matthews	Soccer	England
June 13, 1915	Don Budge	Tennis	United States
February 19, 1916	Eddie Arcaro	Horse racing	United States
June 16, 1916	Hank Luisetti	Basketball	United States
November 21, 1916	Sid Luckman	Football	United States
February 3, 1918	Helen Stephens	Sprints, Shot put, Javelin throw	United States
February 13, 1918	Patty Berg	Golf	United States
August 30, 1918	Ted Williams	Baseball	United States
November 3, 1918	Bob Feller	Baseball	United States
January 31, 1919	Jackie Robinson	Baseball	United States
February 11, 1919	Gretchen Fraser	Skiing	United States
September 28, 1919	Tom Harmon	Football	United States
December 19, 1919	Herb Dudley	Softball	United States
January 6, 1920	Early Wynn	Baseball	United States
January 15, 1920	Bob Davies	Basketball	United States
January 22, 1920	Alf Ramsey	Soccer	England

2911

GREAT ATHLETES

Born	Name	Sport	Country
March 3, 1920	Julius Boros	Golf	United States
June 5, 1920	Marion Motley	Football	United States
July 26, 1920	Bob Waterfield	Football	United States
August 1, 1920	Sammy Lee	Diving	United States
September 6, 1920	Dave Freeman	Badminton	United States
September 22, 1920	Bob Lemon	Baseball	United States
November 21, 1920	Stan Musial	Baseball	United States
December 28, 1920	Steve Van Buren	Football	United States
March 14, 1921	Lis Hartel	Equestrian	Denmark
April 23, 1921	Warren Spahn	Baseball	United States
May 3, 1921	Sugar Ray Robinson	Boxing	United States
August 1, 1921	Jack Kramer	Tennis	United States
August 4, 1921	Maurice "Rocket" Richard	Ice hockey	Canada
August 8, 1921	Betty Shellenberger	Field hockey	United States
October 26, 1921	Joe Fulks	Basketball	United States
November 9, 1921	Victor Tchoukarine	Gymnastics	Soviet Union
November 19, 1921	Roy Campanella	Baseball	United States
December 6, 1921	Otto Graham	Football	United States
January 1, 1922	Rocky Graziano	Boxing	United States
September 19, 1922	Emil Zatopek	Long-distance runs, Marathon	Czechoslovakia
October 27, 1922	Ralph Kiner	Baseball	United States
December 14, 1922	Charley Trippi	Football	United States
June 17, 1923	Elroy "Crazylegs" Hirsch	Football	United States
July 8, 1923	Harrison Dillard	Hurdles	United States
August 8, 1923	Esther Williams	Swimming	United States
August 30, 1923	Vic Seixas	Tennis	United States
September 1, 1923	Rocky Marciano	Boxing	United States
January 25, 1924	Lou Groza	Football	United States
February 6, 1924	Billy Wright	Soccer	England
March 13, 1924	Bertha Tickey	Softball	United States
June 18, 1924	George Mikan	Basketball	United States
November 16, 1924	Mel Patton	Sprints	United States
December 11, 1924	Doc Blanchard	Football	United States
December 23, 1924	Bob Kurland	Basketball	United States
December 26, 1924	Glenn Davis	Football, Hurdles, Sprints	United States
January 4, 1925	Johnny Lujack	Football	United States
February 8, 1925	Raimondo d'Inezeo	Equestrian	Italy
March 26, 1925	Eddie Feigner	Softball	United States
March 29, 1925	Emlen Tunnell	Football	United States
May 1, 1925	Chuck Bednarik	Football	United States
May 12, 1925	Yogi Berra	Baseball	United States
July 18, 1925	Shirley Strickland-de la Hunty	Sprints, Hurdles	Australia
July 29, 1925	Ted Lindsay	Ice hockey	Canada
October 22, 1925	Slater Martin	Basketball	United States
January 21, 1926	Steve Reeves	Bodybuilding	United States
January 23, 1926	Jerry Kramer	Football	United States
February 10, 1926	Danny Blanchflower	Soccer	Northern Ireland
February 20, 1926	Bob Richards	Pole vault, Decathlon	United States

Born	Name	Sport	Country
March 15, 1926	Norm Van Brocklin	Football	United States
May 25, 1926	Bill Sharman	Basketball	United States
July 4, 1926	Alfredo di Stefano	Soccer	Argentina
July 24, 1926	Hans Winkler	Equestrian	Germany
July 29, 1926	Don Carter	Bowling	United States
September 19, 1926	Duke Snider	Baseball	United States
September 30, 1926	Robin Roberts	Baseball	United States
October 3, 1926	Marques Haynes	Basketball	United States
October 24, 1926	Y. A. Tittle	Football	United States
December 6, 1926	Andy Robustelli	Football	United States
December 19, 1926	Bobby Layne	Football	United States
January 1, 1927	Doak Walker	Football	United States
January 2, 1927	Gino Marchetti	Football	United States
August 25, 1927	Althea Gibson	Tennis	United States
September 17, 1927	George Blanda	Football	United States
February 25, 1928	Paul Elvstrøm	Yachting	Denmark
March 31, 1928	Gordie Howe	Ice hockey	Canada
April 9, 1928	Paul Arizin	Basketball	United States
April 16, 1928	Dick "Night Train" Lane	Football	United States
May 9, 1928	Pancho Gonzales	Tennis	United States
May 13, 1928	Jim Shoulders	Rodeo	United States
May 19, 1928	Dolph Schayes	Basketball	United States
August 9, 1928	Bob Cousy	Basketball	United States
October 21, 1928	Whitey Ford	Baseball	United States
December 31, 1928	Hugh McElhenny	Football	United States
January 17, 1929	Jacques Plante	Ice hockey	Canada
March 5, 1929	Casey Tibbs	Rodeo	United States
March 24, 1929	Roger Bannister	Middle-distance runs	England
May 14, 1929	Gump Worsley	Ice hockey	Canada
July 18, 1929	Dick Button	Figure skating	United States
August 14, 1929	Dick Tiger	Boxing	Nigeria
September 7, 1929	Clyde Lovellette	Basketball	United States
September 10, 1929	Arnold Palmer	Golf	United States
October 22, 1929	Lev Yashin	Soccer	Soviet Union
November 24, 1929	John Henry Johnson	Football	United States
December 23, 1929	Dick Weber	Bowling	United States
December 28, 1929	Terry Sawchuk	Ice hockey	Canada
May 8, 1930	Doug Atkins	Football	United States
May 12, 1930	Pat McCormick	Diving	United States
June 27, 1930	Tommy Kono	Weightlifting, Bodybuilding	United States
August 16, 1930	Frank Gifford	Football	United States
August 16, 1930	Tony Trabert	Tennis	United States
November 17, 1930	Bob Mathias	Decathlon	United States
January 31, 1931	Ernie Banks	Baseball	United States
February 16, 1931	Bernie Geoffrion	Ice hockey	Canada
April 13, 1931	Dan Gurney	Auto racing	United States
May 6, 1931	Willie Mays	Baseball	United States
June 24, 1931	Billy Casper	Golf	United States
July 13, 1931	Frank Ramsey	Basketball	United States
August 1, 1931	Harold Connolly	Hammer throw	United States

2913

Born	Name	Sport	Country
August 19, 1931	Willie Shoemaker	Horse racing	United States
August 31, 1931	Jean Beliveau	Ice hockey	Canada
October 3, 1931	Glenn Hall	Ice hockey	Canada
October 13, 1931	Eddie Mathews	Baseball	United States
October 20, 1931	Mickey Mantle	Baseball	United States
December 4, 1931	Alex Delvecchio	Ice hockey	Canada
December 9, 1931	Cliff Hagan	Basketball	United States
January 18, 1932	Joe Schmidt	Football	United States
January 27, 1932	Boris Shakhlin	Gymnastics	Soviet Union
January 28, 1932	Parry O'Brien	Shot put	United States
February 6, 1932	Jim Poole	Badminton	United States
May 25, 1932	K. C. Jones	Basketball	United States
July 16, 1932	Oleg Protopopov	Figure skating	Soviet Union
August 7, 1932	Abebe Bikila	Marathon	Ethiopia
October 2, 1932	Maury Wills	Baseball	United States
October 17, 1932	Paul Anderson	Weightlifting	United States
November 9, 1932	Frank Selvy	Basketball	United States
November 13, 1932	Olga Connolly	Discus throw	Czechoslovakia, United States
November 21, 1932	Jim Ringo	Football	United States
December 9, 1932	Bill Hartack	Horse racing	United States
December 12, 1932	Bob Pettit	Basketball	United States
1933	Garrincha	Soccer	Brazil
January 13, 1933	Tom Gola	Basketball	United States
February 27, 1933	Raymond Berry	Football	United States
February 28, 1933	Chuck Vinci	Weightlifting	United States
May 7, 1933	Johnny Unitas	Football	United States
June 24, 1933	Sam Jones	Basketball	United States
October 18, 1933	Forrest Gregg	Football	United States
November 23, 1933	Carmen Salvino	Bowling	United States
November 25, 1933	Lenny Moore	Football	United States
January 9, 1934	Bart Starr	Football	United States
February 5, 1934	Hank Aaron	Baseball	United States
February 12, 1934	Bill Russell	Basketball	United States
February 20, 1934	Bobby Unser	Auto racing	United States
April 3, 1934	Jim Parker	Football	United States
May 11, 1934	Jack Twyman	Basketball	United States
August 18, 1934	Roberto Clemente	Baseball	Puerto Rico
August 23, 1934	Sonny Jurgensen	Football	United States
August 26, 1934	Tom Heinsohn	Basketball	United States
September 10, 1934	Roger Maris	Baseball	United States
September 16, 1934	Elgin Baylor	Basketball	United States
September 17, 1934	Maureen Connolly	Tennis	United States
October 4, 1934	Sam Huff	Football	United States
October 28, 1934	Jim Beatty	Middle- and long-distance runs	United States
November 2, 1934	Ken Rosewall	Tennis	Australia
November 23, 1934	Lew Hoad	Tennis	Australia
December 19, 1934	Al Kaline	Baseball	United States
December 22, 1934	David Pearson	Auto racing	United States
December 27, 1934	Larisa Latynina	Gymnastics	Soviet Union

Born	Name	Sport	Country
January 4, 1935	Floyd Patterson	Boxing	United States
January 16, 1935	A. J. Foyt	Auto racing	United States
January 25, 1935	Don Maynard	Football	United States
February 14, 1935	Mickey Wright	Golf	United States
May 8, 1935	Jack Charlton	Soccer	England
June 20, 1935	Len Dawson	Football	United States
July 18, 1935	Tenley Albright	Figure skating	United States
July 19, 1935	George Breen	Swimming	United States
August 18, 1935	Rafer Johnson	Decathlon	United States
August 31, 1935	Frank Robinson	Baseball	United States
September 20, 1935	Jim Taylor	Football	United States
October 15, 1935	Bobby Joe Morrow	Sprints	United States
November 1, 1935	Gary Player	Golf	South Africa
November 9, 1935	Bob Gibson	Baseball	United States
November 17, 1935	Toni Sailer	Skiing	Austria
November 22, 1935	Ludmila Protopopov	Figure skating	Soviet Union
December 23, 1935	Paul Hornung	Football	United States
December 30, 1935	Sandy Koufax	Baseball	United States
February 17, 1936	Jim Brown	Football	United States
February 26, 1936	Buddy Werner	Skiing	United States
March 14, 1936	Jim Clark	Auto racing	Scotland
June 26, 1936	Hal Greer	Basketball	United States
June 29, 1936	Harmon Killebrew	Baseball	United States
July 23, 1936	Don Drysdale	Baseball	United States
August 21, 1936	Wilt Chamberlain	Basketball	United States
September 19, 1936	Al Oerter	Discus throw	United States
November 3, 1936	Roy Emerson	Tennis	Australia
December 12, 1936	Iolanda Balas	High jump	Romania
December 23, 1936	Willie Wood	Football	United States
December 29, 1936	Ray Nitschke	Football	United States
March 18, 1937	Mark Donohue	Auto racing	United States
May 18, 1937	Brooks Robinson	Baseball	United States
July 2, 1937	Richard Petty	Auto racing	United States
August 25, 1937	Lones Wigger	Shooting	United States
September 4, 1937	Dawn Fraser	Swimming	Australia
September 16, 1937	Alexander Medved	Wrestling	Soviet Union
October 11, 1937	Bobby Charlton	Soccer	England
October 20, 1937	Juan Marichal	Baseball	Dominican Republic
October 28, 1937	Lenny Wilkens	Basketball	United States
December 3, 1937	Bobby Allison	Auto racing	United States
December 30, 1937	Gordon Banks	Soccer	England
December 30, 1937	Jim Marshall	Football	United States
January 5, 1938	Jim Otto	Football	United States
January 10, 1938	Willie McCovey	Baseball	United States
March 7, 1938	Janet Guthrie	Auto racing	United States
March 10, 1938	Ron Mix	Football	United States
March 12, 1938	Johnny Rutherford	Auto racing	United States
March 24, 1938	Larry Wilson	Football	United States
April 20, 1938	Betty Cuthbert	Sprints	Australia
April 27, 1938	Earl Anthony	Bowling	United States
May 28, 1938	Jerry West	Basketball	United States

2915

GREAT ATHLETES

Born	Name	Sport	Country
June 30, 1938	Billy Mills	Long-distance runs	United States
August 9, 1938	Rod Laver	Tennis	Australia
August 19, 1938	Valentin Mankin	Yachting	Soviet Union
September 15, 1938	Gaylord Perry	Baseball	United States
November 19, 1938	Ted Turner	Yachting	United States
November 24, 1938	Oscar Robertson	Basketball	United States
December 9, 1938	Deacon Jones	Football	United States
December 13, 1938	Gus Johnson	Basketball	United States
December 15, 1938	Bob Foster	Boxing	United States
December 17, 1938	Peter Snell	Middle-distance runs	New Zealand
January 3, 1939	Bobby Hull	Ice hockey	Canada
January 6, 1939	Murray Rose	Swimming	Australia
January 10, 1939	Bill Toomey	Decathlon	United States
March 4, 1939	JoAnne Carner	Golf	United States
March 27, 1939	Cale Yarborough	Auto racing	United States
May 9, 1939	Ralph Boston	Long jump	United States
May 29, 1939	Al Unser	Auto racing	United States
June 8, 1939	Herb Adderley	Football	United States
June 11, 1939	Jackie Stewart	Auto racing	Scotland
June 18, 1939	Lou Brock	Baseball	United States
July 26, 1939	Bob Lilly	Football	United States
August 22, 1939	Carl Yastrzemski	Baseball	United States
September 27, 1939	Kathy Whitworth	Golf	United States
October 11, 1939	Maria Bueno	Tennis	Brazil
October 18, 1939	Mike Ditka	Football	United States
December 1, 1939	Lee Trevino	Golf	United States
December 14, 1939	Ernie Davis	Football	United States
January, 1940	Kip Keino	Long-distance runs	Kenya
January 20, 1940	Carol Heiss	Figure skating	United States
January 21, 1940	Jack Nicklaus	Golf	United States
February 3, 1940	Fran Tarkenton	Football	United States
February 24, 1940	Denis Law	Soccer	Scotland
February 28, 1940	Mario Andretti	Auto racing	Italy, United States
March 30, 1940	Jerry Lucas	Basketball	United States
April 8, 1940	John Havlicek	Basketball	United States
May 10, 1940	Sadaharu Oh	Baseball	Japan
May 20, 1940	Stan Mikita	Ice hockey	Czechoslovakia, Canada
June 11, 1940	Johnny Giles	Soccer	Ireland
June 19, 1940	Shirley Muldowney	Auto racing	United States
June 23, 1940	Wilma Rudolph	Sprints	United States
July 20, 1940	Tony Oliva	Baseball	Cuba
August 3, 1940	Lance Alworth	Football	United States
August 18, 1940	Joan Joyce	Softball	United States
September 10, 1940	Buck Buchanan	Football	United States
September 15, 1940	Merlin Olsen	Football	United States
October 16, 1940	Dave DeBusschere	Basketball	United States
October 23, 1940	Pelé	Soccer	Brazil
December 15, 1940	Nick Buoniconti	Football	United States
January 12, 1941	Chet Jastremski	Swimming	United States
March 6, 1941	Willie Stargell	Baseball	United States

2916

Born	Name	Sport	Country
April 6, 1941	Don Prudhomme	Auto racing	United States
April 12, 1941	Bobby Moore	Soccer	England
April 14, 1941	Pete Rose	Baseball	United States
July 25, 1941	Nate Thurmond	Basketball	United States
December 8, 1941	Geoff Hurst	Soccer	England
January 7, 1942	Vasily Alexeyev	Weightlifting	Soviet Union
January 15, 1942	Carl Eller	Football	United States
January 17, 1942	Muhammad Ali	Boxing	United States
January 25, 1942	Eusebio	Soccer	Mozambique
February 5, 1942	Roger Staubach	Football	United States
February 20, 1942	Phil Esposito	Ice hockey	Canada
April 15, 1942	Walt Hazzard	Basketball	United States
May 3, 1942	Vera Čáslavská	Gymnastics	Czechoslovakia
May 14, 1942	Valery Brumel	High jump	Soviet Union
May 21, 1942	John Konrads	Swimming	Australia
June 25, 1942	Willis Reed	Basketball	United States
July 4, 1942	Floyd Little	Football	United States
July 16, 1942	Margaret Court	Tennis	Australia
July 17, 1942	Connie Hawkins	Basketball	United States
September 4, 1942	Ray Floyd	Golf	United States
September 28, 1942	Charley Taylor	Football	United States
November 8, 1942	Angel Cordero, Jr.	Horse racing	Puerto Rico, United States
November 28, 1942	Paul Warfield	Football	United States
December 9, 1942	Billy Bremner	Soccer	Scotland
December 9, 1942	Dick Butkus	Football	United States
December 20, 1942	Bob Hayes	Sprints, Football	United States
February 23, 1943	Fred Biletnikoff	Football	United States
March 1, 1943	Akinori Nakayama	Gymnastics	Japan
April 13, 1943	Billy Kidd	Skiing	United States
April 23, 1943	Gail Goodrich	Basketball	United States
May 11, 1943	Nancy Greene	Skiing	Canada
May 30, 1943	Gale Sayers	Football	United States
May 31, 1943	Joe Namath	Football	United States
June 3, 1943	Billy Cunningham	Basketball	United States
June 8, 1943	Willie Davenport	Hurdles	United States
July 10, 1943	Arthur Ashe	Tennis	United States
July 28, 1943	Bill Bradley	Basketball	United States
August 30, 1943	Jean-Claude Killy	Skiing	France
September 16, 1943	Dennis Conner	Yachting	United States
September 19, 1943	Joe Morgan	Baseball	United States
September 22, 1943	Jimmie Heuga	Skiing	United States
November 21, 1943	Larry Mahan	Rodeo	United States
November 22, 1943	Billie Jean King	Tennis	United States
November 24, 1943	Dave Bing	Basketball	United States
January 17, 1944	Joe Frazier	Boxing	United States
March 28, 1944	Rick Barry	Basketball	United States
May 23, 1944	John Newcombe	Tennis	Australia
July 26, 1944	Micki King	Diving	United States
November 12, 1944	Ken Houston	Football	United States
November 17, 1944	Tom Seaver	Baseball	United States

Born	Name	Sport	Country
November 21, 1944	Earl Monroe	Basketball	United States
December 22, 1944	Steve Carlton	Baseball	United States
February 3, 1945	Bob Griese	Football	United States
February 18, 1945	Judy Rankin	Golf	United States
February 28, 1945	Bubba Smith	Football	United States
March 5, 1945	Randy Matson	Shot put	United States
March 29, 1945	Walt Frazier	Basketball	United States
May 12, 1945	Alan Ball	Soccer	England
June 3, 1945	Hale Irwin	Golf	United States
June 12, 1945	Pat Jennings	Soccer	Northern Ireland
June 17, 1945	Eddy Merckx	Cycling	Belgium
July 10, 1945	Virginia Wade	Tennis	England
August 7, 1945	Alan Page	Football	United States
August 15, 1945	Gene Upshaw	Football	United States
August 29, 1945	Wyomia Tyus	Sprints	United States
September 11, 1945	Franz Beckenbauer	Soccer	Germany
October 1, 1945	Rod Carew	Baseball	Panama, United States
October 15, 1945	Jim Palmer	Baseball	United States
November 11, 1945	Gerd Müller	Soccer	Germany
November 17, 1945	Elvin Hayes	Basketball	United States
March 6, 1946	Gerry Lindgren	Long-distance runs	United States
March 14, 1946	Wes Unseld	Basketball	United States
April 8, 1946	Catfish Hunter	Baseball	United States
April 30, 1946	Don Schollander	Swimming	United States
May 18, 1946	Reggie Jackson	Baseball	United States
May 22, 1946	George Best	Soccer	Northern Ireland
August 29, 1946	Bob Beamon	Long jump, Triple jump	United States
September 10, 1946	Jim Hines	Sprints, Football	United States
September 24, 1946	Joe Greene	Football	United States
October 11, 1946	Sawao Kato	Gymnastics	Japan
October 17, 1946	Bob Seagren	Pole vault	United States
November 26, 1946	Art Shell	Football	United States
December 12, 1946	Emerson Fittipaldi	Auto racing	Brazil
December 14, 1946	Stan Smith	Tennis	United States
December 25, 1946	Larry Csonka	Football	United States
December 29, 1946	Laffit Pincay, Jr.	Horse racing	Panama, United States
January 31, 1947	Nolan Ryan	Baseball	United States
February 6, 1947	Charlie Hickcox	Swimming	United States
March 6, 1947	Dick Fosbury	High jump	United States
April 16, 1947	Kareem Abdul-Jabbar	Basketball	United States
April 25, 1947	Johan Cruyff	Soccer	The Netherlands
April 26, 1947	Donna de Varona	Swimming	United States
April 29, 1947	Jim Ryun	Middle-distance runs	United States
June 22, 1947	Pete Maravich	Basketball	United States
July 3, 1947	Mike Burton	Swimming	United States
July 9, 1947	O. J. Simpson	Football	United States
July 30, 1947	Arnold Schwarzenegger	Bodybuilding	Austria, United States
August 8, 1947	Ken Dryden	Ice hockey	Canada
August 12, 1947	Linda Metheny	Gymnastics	United States

Born	Name	Sport	Country
September 29, 1947	Corky Carroll	Surfing	United States
October 6, 1947	Klaus Dibiasi	Diving	Italy
October 31, 1947	Frank Shorter	Long-distance runs, Marathon	United States
November 1, 1947	Ted Hendricks	Football	United States
December 7, 1947	Johnny Bench	Baseball	United States
December 22, 1947	Mitsuo Tsukahara	Gymnastics	Japan
December 23, 1947	Bill Rodgers	Long-distance runs, Marathon	United States
January 22, 1948	George Foreman	Boxing	United States
March 20, 1948	Bobby Orr	Ice hockey	Canada
June 4, 1948	Sandra Post	Golf	Canada
July 27, 1948	Peggy Fleming	Figure skating	United States
September 2, 1948	Terry Bradshaw	Football	United States
October 25, 1948	Dan Gable	Wrestling	United States
November 7, 1948	Ivan Yarygin	Wrestling	Soviet Union
December 23, 1948	Jack Ham	Football	United States
December 26, 1948	Carlton Fisk	Baseball	United States
February 22, 1949	Niki Lauda	Auto racing	Austria
July 22, 1949	Lasse Viren	Long-distance runs	Finland
August 13, 1949	Bobby Clarke	Ice hockey	Canada
August 18, 1949	Rudy Hartono	Badminton	Indonesia
September 4, 1949	Tom Watson	Golf	United States
September 9, 1949	John Curry	Figure skating	England
September 12, 1949	Irina Rodnina	Figure skating	Soviet Union
September 18, 1949	Peter Shilton	Soccer	England
September 27, 1949	Mike Schmidt	Baseball	United States
October 20, 1949	Valeri Borzov	Sprints	Soviet Union
October 28, 1949	Bruce Jenner	Decathlon	United States
November 3, 1949	Larry Holmes	Boxing	United States
December 9, 1949	Tom Kite	Golf	United States
February 10, 1950	Mark Spitz	Swimming	United States
February 22, 1950	Julius Erving	Basketball	United States
March 7, 1950	Franco Harris	Football	United States
May 12, 1950	Renate Stecher	Sprints	Germany
May 18, 1950	Rod Milburn	Hurdles	United States
July 27, 1950	Reggie McKenzie	Football	United States
August 5, 1950	Rosi Mittermaier	Skiing	Germany
August 27, 1950	Cynthia Potter	Diving	United States
October 14, 1950	Sheila Young	Speed skating, Cycling	United States
November 8, 1950	Chris Kinard	Badminton	United States
November 13, 1950	Gil Perreault	Ice hockey	Canada
November 15, 1950	Mac Wilkins	Discus throw	United States
November 17, 1950	Roland Matthes	Swimming	Germany
December 20, 1950	Tom Ferguson	Rodeo	United States
December 25, 1950	Kyle Rote, Jr.	Soccer	United States
January 12, 1951	Bill Madlock	Baseball	United States
January 25, 1951	Steve Prefontaine	Long-distance runs	United States
February 25, 1951	Donald Quarrie	Sprints	Jamaica
April 4, 1951	John Hannah	Football	United States
June 16, 1951	Roberto Duran	Boxing	Panama

2919

GREAT ATHLETES

Born	Name	Sport	Country
July 31, 1951	Evonne Goolagong	Tennis	Australia
August 3, 1951	Marcel Dionne	Ice hockey	Canada
September 20, 1951	Guy Lafleur	Ice hockey	Canada
September 25, 1951	Bob McAdoo	Basketball	United States
September 30, 1951	Catie Ball	Swimming	United States
October 3, 1951	Dave Winfield	Baseball	United States
December 3, 1951	Alberto Juantorena	Middle-distance runs	Cuba
December 17, 1951	Tatyana Kazankina	Middle-distance runs	Soviet Union
January 11, 1952	Ben Crenshaw	Golf	United States
January 12, 1952	John Walker	Middle-distance runs	New Zealand
March 7, 1952	Lynn Swann	Football	United States
March 29, 1952	Teófilo Stevenson	Boxing	Cuba
April 16, 1952	Peter Westbrook	Fencing	United States
April 19, 1952	Alexis Arguello	Boxing	Nicaragua, United States
April 25, 1952	Vladislav Tretiak	Ice hockey	Soviet Union
April 27, 1952	George Gervin	Basketball	United States
April 29, 1952	Dale Earnhardt	Auto racing	United States
June 16, 1952	Alexander Zaitsev	Figure skating	Soviet Union
July 8, 1952	Jack Lambert	Football	United States
July 15, 1952	John Stallworth	Football	United States
August 14, 1952	Debbie Meyer	Swimming	United States
August 17, 1952	Guillermo Vilas	Tennis	Argentina
September 2, 1952	Jimmy Connors	Tennis	United States
October 4, 1952	Anita DeFrantz	Rowing	United States
October 7, 1952	Ludmila Turishcheva	Gymnastics	Soviet Union
October 14, 1952	Nikolai Andrianov	Gymnastics	Soviet Union
November 5, 1952	Bill Walton	Basketball	United States
December 12, 1952	Cathy Rigby	Gymnastics	United States
January 10, 1953	Bobby Rahal	Auto racing	United States
January 15, 1953	Randy White	Football	United States
February 17, 1953	Pertti Karppinen	Rowing	Finland
March 27, 1953	Annemarie Moser-Proell	Skiing	Austria
April 6, 1953	Janet Lynn	Figure skating	United States
May 13, 1953	Henry Rono	Long-distance runs, Steeplechase	Kenya
May 15, 1953	George Brett	Baseball	United States
October 1, 1953	Greta Waitz	Marathon	Norway
December 3, 1953	Franz Klammer	Skiing	Austria
December 6, 1953	Dwight Stones	High jump	United States
January 5, 1954	Alex English	Basketball	United States
March 8, 1954	David Wilkie	Swimming	Scotland
April 7, 1954	Tony Dorsett	Football	United States
May 23, 1954	Marvin Hagler	Boxing	United States
July 25, 1954	Walter Payton	Football	United States
July 28, 1954	Steve Zungul	Soccer	Yugoslavia, United States
July 29, 1954	Flo Hyman	Volleyball	United States
August 21, 1954	Archie Griffin	Football	United States
September 28, 1954	Steve Largent	Football	United States
October 3, 1954	Dennis Eckersley	Baseball	United States

Born	Name	Sport	Country
November 14, 1954	Bernard Hinault	Cycling	France
December 21, 1954	Chris Evert	Tennis	United States
December 26, 1954	Susan Butcher	Sled dog racing	United States
1955	Liem Swie-King	Badminton	Indonesia
January 30, 1955	Curtis Strange	Golf	United States
February 10, 1955	Greg Norman	Golf	Australia
February 24, 1955	Alain Prost	Auto racing	France
March 23, 1955	Moses Malone	Basketball	United States
March 26, 1955	Ann Meyers	Basketball	United States
March 27, 1955	Chris McCarron	Horse racing	United States
March 29, 1955	Earl Campbell	Football	United States
April 26, 1955	Mike Scott	Baseball	United States
May 16, 1955	Olga Korbut	Gymnastics	Soviet Union
June 7, 1955	Bill Koch	Skiing	United States
June 21, 1955	Michel Platini	Soccer	France
August 13, 1955	Betsy King	Golf	United States
August 31, 1955	Edwin Moses	Hurdles	United States
September 16, 1955	Robin Yount	Baseball	United States
September 25, 1955	Karl-Heinz Rummenigge	Soccer	Germany
October 9, 1955	Steve Ovett	Middle-distance runs	England
January 20, 1956	John Naber	Swimming	United States
March 11, 1956	Willie Banks	Triple jump	United States
March 12, 1956	Dale Murphy	Baseball	United States
March 18, 1956	Ingemar Stenmark	Skiing	Sweden
March 29, 1956	Kurt Thomas	Gymnastics	United States
May 5, 1956	Steve Scott	Middle-distance runs	United States
May 17, 1956	Sugar Ray Leonard	Boxing	United States
June 6, 1956	Björn Borg	Tennis	Sweden
June 11, 1956	Joe Montana	Football	United States
July 18, 1956	Bryan Trottier	Ice hockey	Canada
July 26, 1956	Dorothy Hamill	Figure skating	United States
September 29, 1956	Sebastian Coe	Middle-distance runs	England
October 18, 1956	Martina Navratilova	Tennis	Czechoslovakia, United States
October 23, 1956	Darrell Pace	Archery	United States
November 23, 1956	Shane Gould	Swimming	Australia
December 7, 1956	Larry Bird	Basketball	United States
December 24, 1956	Lee Kemp	Wrestling	United States
January 2, 1957	Lynne Cox	Swimming	United States
January 6, 1957	Nancy Lopez	Golf	United States
January 22, 1957	Mike Bossy	Ice hockey	Canada
February 19, 1957	Dave Stewart	Baseball	United States
April 2, 1957	Brad Parks	Tennis, Middle-distance runs	United States
April 9, 1957	Seve Ballesteros	Golf	Spain
April 15, 1957	Evelyn Ashford	Sprints	United States
May 10, 1957	Phil Mahre	Skiing	United States
May 16, 1957	Joan Benoit	Marathon	United States
August 7, 1957	Alexander Dityatin	Gymnastics	Soviet Union
August 17, 1957	Robin Cousins	Figure skating	England
October 7, 1957	Jayne Torvill	Figure skating	England

Born	Name	Sport	Country
1958	Yasuhiro Yamashita	Judo	Japan
March 28, 1958	Bart Conner	Gymnastics	United States
June 14, 1958	Eric Heiden	Speed skating	United States
June 15, 1958	Wade Boggs	Baseball	United States
June 25, 1958	Debbie Green	Volleyball	United States
July 1, 1958	Nancy Lieberman-Cline	Basketball	United States
July 27, 1958	Christopher Dean	Figure skating	England
July 30, 1958	Daley Thompson	Decathlon	England
August 4, 1958	Mary Decker-Slaney	Middle- and long-distance runs	United States
August 7, 1958	Alberto Salazar	Marathon	United States
August 24, 1958	Craig Buck	Volleyball	United States
August 28, 1958	Scott Hamilton	Figure skating	United States
September 16, 1958	Orel Hershiser	Baseball	United States
October 1, 1958	Bill Bowness	Waterskiing	United States
October 9, 1958	Mike Singletary	Football	United States
October 18, 1958	Thomas Hearns	Boxing	United States
October 25, 1958	Kornelia Ender	Swimming	Germany
December 2, 1958	Randy Gardner	Figure skating	United States
December 25, 1958	Rickey Henderson	Baseball	United States
February 4, 1959	Lawrence Taylor	Football	United States
February 16, 1959	John McEnroe	Tennis	United States
March 24, 1959	Renaldo Nehemiah	Hurdles, Football	United States
April 2, 1959	Brian Goodell	Swimming	United States
April 19, 1959	Scott Schulte	Water polo	United States
July 24, 1959	Eddie Liddie	Judo	United States
August 12, 1959	Lynette Woodard	Basketball	United States
August 14, 1959	Magic Johnson	Basketball	United States
September 13, 1959	Kathy Johnson	Gymnastics	United States
September 16, 1959	Tim Raines	Baseball	United States
September 18, 1959	Ryne Sandberg	Baseball	United States
December 2, 1959	Greg Barton	Canoeing/Kayaking	United States
December 21, 1959	Florence Griffith-Joyner	Sprints	United States
January 12, 1960	Dominique Wilkins	Basketball	United States
January 29, 1960	Greg Louganis	Diving	United States
January 29, 1960	Steve Sax	Baseball	United States
March 7, 1960	Ivan Lendl	Tennis	Czechoslovakia, United States
May 9, 1960	Tony Gwynn	Baseball	United States
May 21, 1960	Vladimir Salnikov	Swimming	Soviet Union
June 28, 1960	John Elway	Football	United States
July 6, 1960	Valerie Brisco-Hooks	Sprints	United States
August 24, 1960	Cal Ripken, Jr.	Baseball	United States
September 2, 1960	Eric Dickerson	Football	United States
September 22, 1960	Tai Babilonia	Figure skating	United States
October 30, 1960	Diego Maradona	Soccer	Argentina
November 1, 1960	Fernando Valenzuela	Baseball	Mexico
November 3, 1960	Karch Kiraly	Volleyball	United States
November 29, 1960	Howard Johnson	Baseball	United States
November 30, 1960	Gary Lineker	Soccer	England
January 26, 1961	Wayne Gretzky	Ice hockey	Canada, United States

Born	Name	Sport	Country
February 20, 1961	Steve Lundquist	Swimming	United States
March 14, 1961	Kirby Puckett	Baseball	United States
April 20, 1961	Don Mattingly	Baseball	United States
April 30, 1961	Isiah Thomas	Basketball	United States
May 27, 1961	Jon Lugbill	Canoeing/Kayaking	United States
May 27, 1961	Jill Sterkel	Swimming	United States
June 3, 1961	Peter Vidmar	Gymnastics	United States
June 26, 1961	Greg LeMond	Cycling	United States
July 1, 1961	Carl Lewis	Long jump, Sprints	United States
July 4, 1961	Connie Paraskevin-Young	Cycling	United States
November 12, 1961	Nadia Comăneci	Gymnastics	Romania, United States
January 12, 1962	Gunde Svan	Skiing	Sweden
March 3, 1962	Jackie Joyner-Kersee	Heptathlon, Hurdles, Long jump	United States
March 3, 1962	Herschel Walker	Football	United States
March 12, 1962	Darryl Strawberry	Baseball	United States
April 17, 1962	Nancy Hogshead	Swimming	United States
June 22, 1962	Clyde Drexler	Basketball	United States
July 17, 1962	Jay Barrs	Archery	United States
August 4, 1962	Roger Clemens	Baseball	United States
August 26, 1962	Roger Kingdom	Hurdles	United States
October 16, 1962	Tamara McKinney	Skiing	United States
November 30, 1962	Bo Jackson	Baseball, Football	United States
January 11, 1963	Tracy Caulkins	Swimming	United States
January 11, 1963	Petra Schneider	Swimming	Germany
January 21, 1963	Hakeem Olajuwon	Basketball	United States
February 4, 1963	Tracie Ruiz-Conforto	Synchronized swimming	United States
February 4, 1963	Pirmin Zurbriggen	Skiing	Switzerland
February 17, 1963	Michael Jordan	Basketball	United States
March 20, 1963	Diana Golden	Skiing	United States
July 17, 1963	Matti Nykänen	Ski jumping	Finland
October 22, 1963	Brian Boitano	Figure skating	United States
December 14, 1963	Sergei Bubka	Pole vault	Soviet Union
January 3, 1964	Cheryl Miller	Basketball	United States
February 7, 1964	Cynthia Woodhead	Swimming	United States
March 13, 1964	Will Clark	Baseball	United States
March 18, 1964	Bonnie Blair	Speed skating	United States
April 11, 1964	Bret Saberhagen	Baseball	United States
July 2, 1964	José Canseco	Baseball	Cuba, United States
July 3, 1964	Tom Curren	Surfing	United States
October 27, 1964	Mary T. Meagher	Swimming	United States
December 5, 1964	Pablo Morales	Swimming	United States
August 6, 1965	David Robinson	Basketball	United States
October 5, 1965	Mario Lemieux	Ice hockey	Canada
October 8, 1965	Matt Biondi	Swimming	United States
October 11, 1965	Julianne McNamara	Gymnastics	United States
October 28, 1965	Martin Potter	Surfing	South Africa, Australia
December 3, 1965	Katarina Witt	Figure skating	Germany
January 19, 1966	Stefan Edberg	Tennis	Sweden

2923

GREAT ATHLETES

Born	Name	Sport	Country
June 30, 1966	Mike Tyson	Boxing	United States
August 27, 1966	Deena Wigger	Shooting	United States
January 23, 1967	Naim Suleymanoglu	Weightlifting	Bulgaria, Turkey
November 22, 1967	Boris Becker	Tennis	Germany
January 24, 1968	Mary Lou Retton	Gymnastics	United States
June 14, 1969	Steffi Graf	Tennis	Germany
May 16, 1970	Gabriela Sabatini	Tennis	Argentina
August 28, 1971	Janet Evans	Swimming	United States
February 9, 1973	Svetlana Boginskaya	Gymnastics	Soviet Union
December 2, 1973	Monica Seles	Tennis	Yugoslavia
December 12, 1973	Denise Parker	Archery	United States

GREAT ATHLETES

THE
TWENTIETH
CENTURY

Name Index

V

Duke Snider **17**-2367
Warren Spahn **17**-2371
Tris Speaker **17**-2375
Willie Stargell **17**-2387
Casey Stengel **17**-2407
Dave Stewart **17**-2427
Darryl Strawberry **17**-2443
Bill Terry **17**-2489
Jim Thorpe **18**-2506
Pie Traynor **18**-2555
Fernando Valenzuela **18**-2627
Dazzy Vance **19**-2638
Rube Waddell **19**-2666
Honus Wagner **19**-2673
Ted Williams **19**-2771
Maury Wills **19**-2775
Hack Wilson **20**-2779
Dave Winfield **20**-2786
Early Wynn **20**-2825
Carl Yastrzemski **20**-2845
Cy Young **20**-2849
Robin Yount **20**-2857

BASKETBALL

Kareem Abdul-Jabbar **1**-5
Paul Arizin **1**-74
Rick Barry **2**-145
Elgin Baylor **2**-157
Dave Bing **2**-222
Larry Bird **2**-230
Bill Bradley **2**-293
Wilt Chamberlain **3**-419
Bob Cousy **4**-516
Billy Cunningham **4**-544
Bob Davies **4**-564
Dave DeBusschere **4**-585
Clyde Drexler **5**-651
Alex English **5**-711
Julius Erving **5**-715
Walt Frazier **6**-811
Joe Fulks **6**-819
George Gervin **6**-843
Tom Gola **6**-867
Gail Goodrich **6**-886
Hal Greer **7**-929
Cliff Hagan **7**-977
John Havlicek **7**-1029
Connie Hawkins **7**-1033
Elvin Hayes **8**-1041
Marques Haynes **8**-1045
Walt Hazzard **8**-1048

Tom Heinsohn **8**-1061
Gus Johnson **9**-1189
Magic Johnson **9**-1213
K. C. Jones **9**-1232
Sam Jones **9**-1236
Michael Jordan **9**-1240
Bob Kurland **10**-1368
Joe Lapchick **10**-1395
Nancy Lieberman-Cline **10**-1467
Clyde Lovellette **11**-1513
Jerry Lucas **11**-1517
Hank Luisetti **11**-1529
Bob McAdoo **11**-1544
Moses Malone **11**-1593
Pete Maravich **11**-1612
Slater Martin **12**-1643
Ann Meyers **12**-1707
George Mikan **12**-1711
Cheryl Miller **12**-1723
Earl Monroe **12**-1743
Hakeem Olajuwon **13**-1885
Bob Pettit **14**-1991
Frank Ramsey **14**-2067
Willis Reed **15**-2075
Oscar Robertson **15**-2109
David Robinson **15**-2117
Bill Russell **15**-2180
Dolph Schayes **16**-2249
Frank Selvy **16**-2303
Bill Sharman **16**-2311
Isiah Thomas **17**-2493
Nate Thurmond **18**-2510
Jack Twyman **18**-2595
Wes Unseld **18**-2611
Bill Walton **19**-2696
Jerry West **19**-2724
Lenny Wilkens **19**-2751
Dominique Wilkins **19**-2759
Lynette Woodard **20**-2801
John Wooden **20**-2805
Babe Didrikson Zaharias **20**-2861

BOBSLEDDING

Eddie Eagan **5**-672

BODYBUILDING

Tommy Kono **10**-1346
Steve Reeves **15**-2079
Eugen Sandow **16**-2229
Arnold Schwarzenegger **16**-2275

BOWLING

Earl Anthony **1**-57
Don Carter **3**-402
Marion Ladewig **10**-1375
Floretta Doty McCutcheon **11**-1560
Carmen Salvino **16**-2221
Dick Weber **19**-2712

BOXING

Muhammad Ali **1**-29
Alexis Arguello **1**-69
Henry Armstrong **1**-82
Max Baer **1**-106
Jack Dempsey **5**-605
Roberto Duran **5**-667
Eddie Eagan **5**-672
George Foreman **6**-779
Bob Foster **6**-787
Joe Frazier **6**-807
Rocky Graziano **7**-909
Marvin Hagler **7**-985
Thomas Hearns **8**-1052
Larry Holmes **8**-1116
Jack Johnson **9**-1197
Sugar Ray Leonard **10**-1450
Joe Louis **11**-1509
Rocky Marciano **11**-1623
Archie Moore **12**-1756
Floyd Patterson **14**-1960
Sugar Ray Robinson **15**-2129
Max Schmeling **16**-2253
Teófilo Stevenson **17**-2423
Dick Tiger **18**-2522
Gene Tunney **18**-2583
Mike Tyson **18**-2599

BROAD JUMP

Jim Thorpe **18**-2506

CANOEING/KAYAKING

Greg Barton **2**-149
Jon Lugbill **11**-1525

CRICKET

Donald G. Bradman **2**-297
Learie Constantine **4**-500

SOFTBALL
Herb Dudley **5**-663
Eddie Feigner **6**-747
Joan Joyce **9**-1245
Bertha Tickey **18**-2518
Babe Didrikson Zaharias **20**-2861

 SPEED SKATING
Bonnie Blair **2**-234
Eric Heiden **8**-1057
Sheila Young **20**-2853

SPRINTS
Harold Abrahams **1**-9
Evelyn Ashford **1**-91
Valeri Borzov **2**-278
Valerie Brisco-Hooks **3**-317
Betty Cuthbert **4**-556
Glenn Davis **4**-572
Florence Griffith-Joyner **7**-949
Bob Hayes **7**-1037
Jim Hines **8**-1096
Carl Lewis **10**-1455
Eric Liddell **10**-1460
Bobby Joe Morrow **12**-1776
Jesse Owens **13**-1919
Charles Paddock **13**-1927
Mel Patton **14**-1964
Donald Quarrie **14**-2051
Wilma Rudolph **15**-2165
Renate Stecher **17**-2399
Helen Stephens **17**-2415
Shirley Strickland-de la Hunty
    17-2447
Eddie Tolan **18**-2534
Wyomia Tyus **18**-2603

STEEPLECHASE
Paavo Nurmi **13**-1865
Henry Rono **15**-2145

 SURFING
Corky Carroll **3**-399
Tom Curren **4**-548
Duke Kahanamoku **9**-1261
Martin Potter **14**-2027

SWIMMING
Catie Ball **1**-119
Matt Biondi **2**-226
Ethelda Bleibtrey **2**-250
George Breen **3**-305
Mike Burton **3**-355
Tracy Caulkins **3**-414
Lynne Cox **4**-524
Buster Crabbe **4**-528
Donna de Varona **5**-609
Gertrude Ederle **5**-687
Kornelia Ender **5**-707
Janet Evans **5**-727
Dawn Fraser **6**-799
Brian Goodell **6**-882
Shane Gould **6**-894
Charlie Hickcox **8**-1088
Nancy Hogshead **8**-1112
Chet Jastremski **8**-1177
Duke Kahanamoku **9**-1261
John Konrads **10**-1350
Steve Lundquist **11**-1536
Roland Matthes **12**-1663
Mary T. Meagher **12**-1683
Debbie Meyer **12**-1703
Pablo Morales **12**-1768
John Naber **13**-1810
Martha Norelius **13**-1858
Murray Rose **15**-2149
Vladimir Salnikov **16**-2217
Petra Schneider **16**-2264
Don Schollander **16**-2267
Mark Spitz **17**-2379
Jill Sterkel **17**-2419
Johnny Weissmuller **19**-2716
David Wilkie **19**-2755
Esther Williams **19**-2767
Cynthia Woodhead **20**-2809

 **SYNCHRONIZED
SWIMMING**
Tracie Ruiz-Conforto **15**-2173

TENNIS
Arthur Ashe **1**-87
Boris Becker **2**-172
Björn Borg **2**-266
Jean Borotra **2**-274
Don Budge **3**-344

Maria Bueno **3**-348
Henri Cochet **4**-461
Maureen Connolly **4**-488
Jimmy Connors **4**-496
Margaret Court **4**-507
Stefan Edberg **5**-683
Roy Emerson **5**-703
Chris Evert **5**-735
Althea Gibson **6**-847
Pancho Gonzales **6**-878
Evonne Goolagong **6**-890
Steffi Graf **7**-897
Lew Hoad **8**-1104
Billie Jean King **9**-1319
Jack Kramer **10**-1361
René Lacoste **10**-1371
Rod Laver **10**-1411
Ivan Lendl **10**-1438
Suzanne Lenglen **10**-1442
John McEnroe **11**-1567
Alice Marble **11**-1616
Helen Wills Moody **12**-1752
Martina Navratilova **13**-1830
John Newcombe **13**-1846
Brad Parks **14**-1956
Fred Perry **14**-1983
Ken Rosewall **15**-2157
Gabriela Sabatini **15**-2201
Vic Seixas **16**-2295
Monica Seles **16**-2299
Stan Smith **16**-2355
Bill Tilden **18**-2526
Tony Trabert **18**-2551
Guillermo Vilas **19**-2654
Virginia Wade **19**-2669
Hazel Wightman **19**-2747

TRIPLE JUMP
Willie Banks **1**-133
Bob Beamon **2**-161
Ray Ewry **5**-739

VOLLEYBALL
Craig Buck **3**-341
Debbie Green **7**-913
Flo Hyman **8**-1159
Karch Kiraly **10**-1330

WATER POLO
Scott Schulte **16**-2271

XIV

WATERSKIING
Bill Bowness **2**-290

 WEIGHTLIFTING
Vasily Alexeyev **1**-25
Paul Anderson **1**-41

Tommy Kono **10**-1346
Naim Suleymanoglu **17**-2451
Chuck Vinci **19**-2658

 WRESTLING
Dan Gable **6**-823
Lee Kemp **9**-1292

Alexander Medved **12**-1687
Ivan Yarygin **20**-2837

 YACHTING
Dennis Conner **4**-481
Paul Elvstrøm **5**-695
Valentin Mankin **11**-1601
Ted Turner **18**-2591

XVIII

XIX